*THE ISLANDS SERIES*

# GIBRALTAR

*Other titles in the Islands Series*

# GIBRALTAR

by *PHILIP DENNIS*

DAVID & CHARLES

NEWTON ABBOT  LONDON  NORTH POMFRET (VT)

ISBN 0 7153 7358 7


First published 1977
Second impression 1979
Third impression 1985

© PHILIP DENNIS 1977

Printed in Great Britain by
Redwood Burn Ltd Trowbridge Wiltshire
for David & Charles (Publishers) Limited
Brunel House Newton Abbot Devon

Published in the United States of America
by David & Charles Inc
North Pomfret Vermont 05053 USA

# CONTENTS

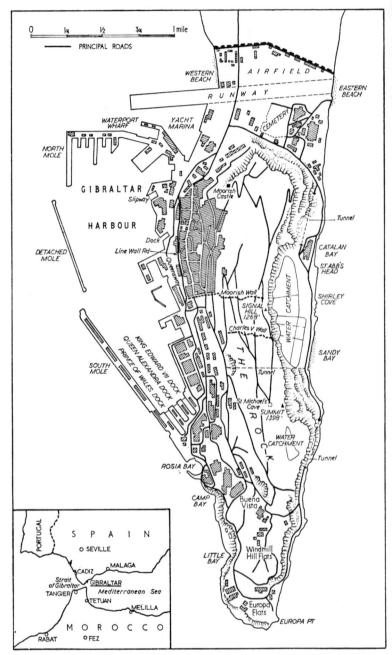

Sketch map of 'The Rock' based on that of Service Publications Ltd

# INTRODUCTION

A HUMAN skull was found in a quarry on the Rock of Gibraltar in 1848. At that time no great significance was attached to the discovery, but 8 years later a similar skull was found in the Neanderthal valley in Germany; then it was realised that human history in Gibraltar went back a very long way to a type of man now known as Neanderthal. In much later times the Phoenicians, the Greeks and the Romans were interested in the Rock simply as a landmark. The Romans knew it as Mons Calpe, one of the pillars of Hercules; the other was Mount Abyla on the opposite side of the Straits of Gibraltar, now known in Gibraltar as Apes' Hill.

The name Gibraltar is a corruption of Gebel Tarik, meaning Tarik's mountain, after the Moorish commander who led the invasion of southern Spain in 711. The Moors were finally expelled from the Rock in 1462 and it remained in Spanish hands until 1704. In that year a British and Dutch force captured it and in 1713 it was ceded to Britain by the Treaty of Utrecht. The Rock was a valuable military asset for Britain in the Napoleonic Wars and the two world wars, but its retention has cost much loss of Spanish goodwill.

For defenders the Rock has great natural advantages. The eastern side is almost inaccessible, with a steep descent to the sea from the ridge that forms the summit. The highest point, 1,396ft (425·5m) above sea level, is towards the southern end. From here there is a steep slope down to Windmill Hill at a height of 400ft (122m), followed by a similar descent to Europa Flats at a height of 100ft (30·5m). These two areas are level platforms above cliffs around Europa Point. The western side has offered the only practicable approach from the sea

7

during Gibraltar's history, but even here the slopes favour the defenders. The northern face is an almost vertical cliff rising over 1,300ft (396m) above the sandy isthmus that forms a land bridge with Spain about 10ft (3·05m) above sea level.

The Rock is 3 miles (4·8km) long from Europa Point to its northern face and the British boundary stands $\frac{1}{2}$ mile (805m) away across the isthmus, which is about $\frac{1}{2}$ mile wide. The total area inside the boundary is about $2\frac{1}{4}$ square miles (583 hectares). The latitude of Gibraltar, which was determined with a fair degree of accuracy by Ptolemy, is 36° 7′ North, and the longitude is 5° 21′ West. It is thus at approximately the same latitude as Malta, Crete and Cyprus, and almost due south of Cape Wrath and The Lizard.

The most interesting approach to Gibraltar is by sea through the Straits. The opening of the Suez Canal in 1869 led to the development of Gibraltar as a port on the sea route to the Far East, but it was busiest during the years between the world wars, when ocean liners called with a regularity comparable to that of airliners today, although not, of course, with the same frequency. The P & O, for example, called homeward-bound on Mondays and outward-bound on Tuesdays.

Travellers today on cruise ships, or on the Bland Line cross-channel ship *Mons Calpe* from Tangier, still get the same view. The Rock gradually appears through the mist, resembling a crouching lion; in former times this view of the guardian of the Straits epitomised British sea power, with its chain of bases through the Mediterranean, the Suez Canal and the Red Sea to Aden, Trincomalee, Singapore and Hong Kong.

As the Rock comes nearer, it gradually dominates the scene, its barren-looking light-grey limestone, almost white in appearance, tempered by some green areas of olive trees and shrub. The green provides a welcome relief from the glare of the limestone and light-coloured buildings on the western slopes. On the Spanish shores of the Bay of Gibraltar there are rounded hills that look brown where they are not covered with vegetation. The bay is enclosed on the eastern, northern and western shores, but it can be badly affected by south-westerly gales, which sometimes blow through the Straits in winter. The western side of the bay ends at Carnero Point from where the coast assumes a west-south-westerly direction to Tarifa Point, the most southerly place on the mainland of Europe.

In the foreground, when one is approaching the Rock, lies the naval harbour, covering an area of 440 acres (178 hectares). During the world wars the harbour and the bay attained their greatest activity as a convoy-collecting area; and between the wars Gibraltar was a meeting place for ships of the Home and Mediterranean Fleets on spring manoeuvres. Now fewer and smaller ships have replaced the large battle fleets composed of ships with famous names like *Hood*, *Rodney* and *Nelson*; and they now often belong to several NATO countries.

Most travellers to Gibraltar arrive by air. The airport built for the RAF during World War II is on the isthmus and half the runway extends out into the sea to a total length of 2,000yd (1,829m). Landing at most airports is very dull, but at Gibraltar the traveller with a window seat gets an excellent view of the Rock, and if the landing is from the east, the sheer cliff of the north face can be seen alongside the aircraft.

When a traveller alights at the airport buildings, he will find a scene similar to the arrival of aircraft at an offshore island, but in this case the direct flights from Britain cover over 1,200 miles (1,930km). The flights bring servicemen and their families, businessmen and tourists. The airport buildings lie in an area occupied by besieging forces in most of the fourteen sieges; tarmac now covers the sand, but it is easy to understand how small the besiegers must have felt below the towering Rock. The keep of the Moorish Castle flying the Union flag stands out behind a modern housing estate; most of its history belongs to days before the British capture of the Rock.

The town of Gibraltar is about $\frac{1}{2}$ mile (805m) from the airport and stands on the western slopes of the Rock. Main Street, the chief shopping area, runs for nearly a mile from north to south. Above Main Street lines of buildings rise in tiers for $\frac{1}{4}$ mile (400m) up the slopes of the Rock along parallel streets joined by narrow lanes and steps.

The buildings are mixed in style. The use of Spanish tiles and other building materials as well as the louvred shutters in front of windows gives a Spanish flavour to some of the architecture, but there are also old military quarters in eighteenth- and nineteenth-century British style, together with modern banks and supermarkets. The telephone booths, post boxes and taverns are unmistakably British, and the Victorian-style police station houses a force indistinguishable from British policemen. Their bearing and courtesy are similar and they speak English perfectly, although they may talk in Spanish among themselves. Traffic travels on the right-hand side of the road, so the Gibraltar police are among the few British police with this experience. The system was adopted in the days when the frontier with Spain was freely left open.

The Spanish frontier, lying about 200yd (183m) north of the airport, was closed to all persons in 1969. This has caused great hardship to many Gibraltarians who have relatives in Spain, as a visit to Spain now, via Tangier and Algeciras, means covering a distance of about 100 miles (161km).

At the time of the census of 1970 the total population was 27,965. This has now increased to about 30,000, including 3,000 Moroccans, who have replaced the Spanish workers prevented from crossing the frontier.

There are about 20,000 Gibraltarians with long-established family roots in Gibraltar, whose ancestors came from many countries, including Britain, Italy, Portugal and Malta as well as Spain, and they are at the centre of the controversy with Spain over sovereignty. Spain claims that the Rock should be returned as part of the decolonisation process proclaimed by the United Nations Organisation. Gibraltar is not a geographical island, but its history and its people are distinct. The closure of the Spanish frontier has made the people more isolated than many islanders.

Such recent developments, however, need to be considered against the background of history. The natural strategic strength of the Rock has played a large part in its history, so its physical features will be considered first. Too much emphasis on current events needs to be avoided. Disputes often settle themselves in time, and it is more useful to study the place as it is, its history, its people and the relation of these to each other and the outside world.

# 1                                  INSIDE THE ROCK

GIBRALTAR forms part of the mountain system of southern Spain known as the Betic Cordillera, which stretches from the Atlantic coast in the area around Cadiz to Cap de la Nao, north-east of Alicante. The Balearic Islands are part of the same system, and the mountain-building process of the Tertiary Era in geological time extended to the Atlas mountains in North Africa. The exact way in which the Rock fits into the geomorphology of the area is not known. The inside of the Rock has, however, been studied in the course of military tunnelling and in the search for water supplies.

The main mass of the Rock is composed of limestone laid down beneath the sea in the Jurassic Period. The limestone of the Rock is overlaid on the western side by shale and loose sand; there are also some small outcrops of shale on the eastern side. To the west of the Rock the shale beds in turn dip under sandstone beneath the Bay of Gibraltar.

## THE LIMESTONE MOUNTAIN

The sedimentary rock formation of this period took place between 135 and 180 million years ago during the Secondary Era before the mountain building started. The neighbouring mountains and hills in Spain are predominantly composed of sandstone, but limestone reappears on the other side of the Straits in Apes' Hill, the southern Pillar of Hercules.

The detachment of Europe from North Africa is probably the result of an overspill eroding a passage between the Atlantic and the Mediterranean. Variations in sea levels in the area are illustrated by the raised beaches around the Rock itself. Europa Flats are the most marked example of a raised beach, but marine deposits provide evidence of such beaches at a number of different levels. In the Europa area the levels vary between 30ft (9·14m) and 140ft (42·67m). At the northern end of the Rock there is a similar type of terrace at a height of about 150ft (45·72m), where the defences known as Prince's Lines were built during the eighteenth century.

Limestones of the Jurassic Period occur in many other parts of Europe, including Britain, where they form part of the Jurassic scarplands extending from the Dorset to the north Yorkshire coast. The limestones often underlie other rocks, but they appear on the surface in such places as Portland Bill. Both limestone and chalk consist of calcium carbonate of varying degrees of purity, but limestone is harder and forms in beds. Both stand out prominently in relief on the land-scape, as they absorb the surface drainage. Another important form of rock composed of calcium carbonate is marble, which occurs in the Sierra Nevada about 120 miles (193km) north-east of Gibraltar. Marble and calcite are crystalline forms of calcium carbonate, and the latter can be seen in places on the Rock in bands of varying thickness up to 3ft (91·4cm).

The surface rocks and soil consist of limestone, shale, Alameda sand and sand with gravel. There is a main fault which runs in a south-easterly direction from near the end of South Mole, through the northern edge of Windmill Hill, to the sea about ½ mile (805m) north of Europa Point. There are many other smaller faults, some of which run almost at right-angles to the great main fault, but the striking feature of the main fault is the reversal of the dip of the beds on the southern side. This can clearly be seen when one looks north-wards from Europa Point, in the contrast between the dip at the top of the Rock and on Windmill Hill.

Superficial deposits include older limestone breccia, which can be seen around Rosia Bay and South Barracks, and more recent breccia, to be found on marine-eroded terraces and among the Catalan Bay sands on the eastern side of the Rock. The sands have been blown up from the shore to become bedded in some places, and form part of the talus with the limestone broken off from the Rock. Much of the breaking away of pieces of the main mass of limestone mountain occurred when the Rock was subjected to frost in the Quaternary Ice Ages.

Perhaps the most important of the superficial deposits are the Alameda Sands, which are red siliceous sands of an incoherent nature, and are called the Red Sands in descriptions of the sieges. They occur in the area of the town and more markedly in the Alameda Gardens, where they provide fertile soil. The sands extend up the Rock as much as 170ft (51·82m) above sea level. In the town they form only a thin cover in places above the shales, which provide the foundation for the buildings. The thicker sands in the Alameda Gardens area have provided a source of water in the past from wells sunk down to the impervious shale beds. The wells still remaining have a high degree of salinity, but an old Spanish aqueduct to the town indicates their importance in earlier times.

The limestone beds forming the main mass of the Rock vary in thickness from a few feet to several yards. There is well marked jointing in the limestone, and this has allowed water to percolate and cause a slow process of dissolution of the rock. Limestone is only slightly soluble in water, but over a long period channels form in it. These channels sometimes open out into large caves, as has happened in Britain – for example, in the limestones of the Pennines and the Mendips – and there are many such caves in the limestone of the Rock.

### THE CAVES

St Michael's cave, known to man for about 2,000 years but formed over millions of years, is a striking example of a limestone cave. The entrance is 900ft (274·32m) above sea level and it opens out into a large dome-shaped cavern, 70ft (21·34m) high, known as the Cathedral. This has now been developed as a tourist attraction, and the fine acoustic properties have been used for a variety of musical performances. The idea of making use of the cave was first put into effect during World War II, when it was fitted out as a hospital, although not used as such. The excavations resulted in the discovery of yet another cave, now known as Lower St Michael's cave.

It was perhaps easier before any developments occurred to appreciate the great natural beauty of St Michael's cave, with its fine stalactite and stalagmite formations, which have joined together in many places to give the impression of the pillars of a cathedral. The formation of these pillars by the slow evaporation of water containing calcium carbonate to form calcite is a geological process still going on, although a very slow one.

Small passages and tunnels lead off from the main Cathedral of St Michael's cave. Excavations were begun in 1840 by Captain Webber-Smith. Two officers were thought to have disappeared in the cave a few years earlier, but no traces of them have been found in any later explorations, though they have gone down several hundred feet. The passages that have been explored are very wet, with water trickling through them, and give an impression of the Rock as a hard sponge, so that the expression 'as solid as the Rock of Gibraltar' is not altogether well chosen.

St Michael's cave is an example of a cave eroded by the action of water falling as rainfall. There is more interest from a human historical point of view in the second type of cave, in which sea erosion has played a part; these occur around the present coastline and on raised beaches. There are seven such caves about ¾ mile (1·21km) north of Europa Point below Europa Advance Road. One of these is called Gorham's cave after the name of the officer who first explored it in 1907. Since 1948 much further excavation has been carried out in this cave, which was filled with sand to a height of 50ft (15·24m) above sea level; and a study has been made of findings in different layers, though some material still awaits analysis. Pottery, jewellery and glassware show that the Phoenicians visited the cave from about 800 BC. They did not inhabit the Rock, but they revered it and probably left offerings to help ensure the success of their missions beyond the Pillars of Hercules, which were the subject of much mythology; some thought in ancient times that the world ended not far beyond them.

Altogether there are over 100 caves. Bones found in them and among rocks and crevices show that large animals such as the bear, leopard, lynx, wolf, hyena and rhinoceros once lived on the Rock. Human habitation goes back to Neanderthal man. The original finding of a skull of this age in 1848 was followed by the finding of another skull in 1926 – a child's skull, discovered not far from the site of the earlier finding. Both the Old and the New Stone Ages are represented in finds in caves.

It is perhaps surprising to find so much evidence of very early human history, but a comparatively late arrival of man on the scene in historical times. The vegetation was probably more luxuriant in earlier times, so that it supported animals that man could hunt. A more important consideration, however, probably concerns water. A few cave-dwellers could have found enough water in the caves, but agricultural settlements of historical times required more than trickles in caves. The Phoenicians and Romans were therefore much better placed in Carteia, at the mouth of the Guadarranque river about 5 miles (8km) north-west of Gibraltar, than on Gibraltar itself.

### THE WATER SUPPLY

During the past 100 years the trickles of water running through caves have given rise to much speculation over whether a useful supply might be obtained out of the limestone. Unfortunately there is no impervious layer of other rock below the limestone and above sea level. In the area around the great main fault a well has been sunk and a small amount of water obtained, but otherwise getting water out of the limestone has proved most elusive. As long ago as 1889 Major Tulloch of the Royal Engineers put forward the theory that above a certain point near sea level the Rock is saturated with fresh water, while below this it is saturated with sea water, and it should be possible to trap the lighter fresh water where it is still floating on the heavier salt water. Interest in this theory has recently been revived, but neither infra-red surveys nor the use of tracer dyes has revealed any large out-flow of water. An additional problem over isolating fresh water near sea level arises from the use of sea water for sanitary purposes, including washing the streets, and there is also pollution from occasional spillage of hydrocarbon oils from pipe lines in tunnels within the Rock.

As a total of 30 miles (48·28km) of tunnel have been excavated in the Rock, it would seem that at least one large source of water might have been found by chance, if any such sources exist. It is perhaps more probable that there are many gentle trickles. Consequently the isthmus may remain the only area where supplies of fresh water in useful quantities can be obtained. In 1865 the Sanitary Commissioners set to work there, soon after their appointment, trying to find water near the north face of the Rock; and in 1869 there was a ceremonial opening of a new piped supply in Commercial Square (now John Mackintosh Square), but the water turned saline owing to excessive pumping. A further attempt to obtain fresh-water supplies was made in 1876, when Ramsay and Geikie made the first scientific geological survey of the Rock and the isthmus – a most valuable piece of work – but only brackish water was found on the isthmus, where it was resting on a clay layer about 30ft (9·14m) below the surface. Water from this and other wells sunk on the isthmus was used until after World War II for washing and sanitary purposes.

Soon after Ramsay and Geikie left, the quest for fresh water was abandoned, but in 1935 borings made near the British boundary were successful in obtaining fresh-water supplies at a depth of about 15ft (4·57m) below a sandstone layer. Now about 35 million gallons are obtained each year from wells, supplying about a quarter of Gibraltar's requirements. The water is analysed for chloride content, and some slightly salt water is blended with supplies from catchments and distillation plants.

The town supply of drinking water is based upon thirteen reservoirs, built inside the Rock, with a capacity of 16 million gallons. Building began on the first reservoir shortly before the end of the nineteenth century, and in 1903 the first catchment on the east side of the Rock was built. The catchment area now covers over 30 acres (12·15 hectares) and it can be seen for many miles away at sea. The system of construction consisted of driving wooden supports into the sands, which are sufficiently consolidated to form a good anchorage; fitting cross-members on top of the supports; attaching iron sheets to the framework; and covering the sheets with a thin cement wash. The structure is still the same, maintenance being mostly carried out during the dry summers. When rain falls on the catchment, it runs into a channel at the base, which leads into a tunnel through the Rock. The tunnel comes out just above Moorish Castle, and thirteen reservoirs excavated out of the Rock and lined with non-porous material lie at right-angles to the tunnel.

A third source of drinking water consists of three distillation plants using sea water: the smallest uses waste heat from the power station, another near the eastern beach is a multi-stage flash evaporator, and the newest in the harbour area is a vertical tube evaporator. Distilled water is used as necessary to supplement well water and rain water. Distillation has become a much more expensive process since the rise in oil prices from the end of 1973 onwards. A further emergency source of water is importation by tanker, but except when there is unusual drought or demand, the catchments, the wells and the distillation plants supply Gibraltar's needs.

Water from wells and the distillation plants is pumped to a central pumping station (just outside Landport gate) known as Hesse's station after the name of the old bastion in which it stands. From here the water is pumped to the reservoirs, where the blend from the catchments, wells and distillation is made. Since World War II great progress has been made in the distribution system, and houses and flats now have supplies of sea water for sanitary purposes and potable water for drinking and washing. Before World War II only half the dwellings had any fresh supply, and brackish water was used for washing in all houses. There were central supply points for fresh water then, and it was common to see Spanish vendors in the streets with barrels of water slung on donkeys.

# 2    CLIMATE AND NATURAL FEATURES

NATURE has not been so unkind to Gibraltar as the lack of fertile land and problems over water might suggest. The climate is a pleasant Mediterranean one with abundant sunshine. Even December, the month with the lowest daily average, has over 5 hours a day, and July, the sunniest month, has over 11 hours a day. The sunshine is greatly appreciated by people from more northern climates, and it is now probably Gibraltar's greatest economic asset.

### DRY SUMMERS AND TEMPERATE WINTERS

The seasons are normally classified as spring from March to May, summer from June to August, autumn from September to November, and winter from December to February, though a more important division of the year is that between the dry and the rainy seasons. The summer months are almost rainless, and the rainy season generally extends from the latter part of September to the end of May. The year for the purpose of rainfall measurements runs from September to the end of the following August. Measurements have been kept since 1790, but different stations have been used at different periods, so variations in averages have no climatic significance. The most recent annual figure from RAF observations over 42 years is 31·9in (810mm), almost exactly the same as the figure for the years 1790 to 1840. The maximum recorded in a year is 78in (1,980mm) and the minimum is 15in (381mm). November, December and January are the wettest months and on average 5–6in (127–152mm) fall in each of them. This accounts for half the year's rainfall, and much of the remainder falls between February and April. There are large variations from year to year in the months in which rain falls as well as in the total rainfall, but the dry weather from June to August is only broken by an occasional heavy shower.

Much of the rain is caused by troughs associated with Atlantic depressions, the rain usually coming with westerly winds and much of it falling in heavy showers. On average the whole of the annual rainfall occurs on only eighty-five days. Snow is almost unknown, but heavy hailstorms sometimes occur; they are rare, but there were three in May 1972.

August is the warmest month, with an average daily mean temperature of 75° F (23.9° C), and January the coldest, with a corresponding temperature of 55° F (12.8° C). The maritime influence prevents extremes of temperature in either summer or winter. The average daily maximum in August is 82° F (27.7° C). The maximum recorded since 1930 is 101° F (39.3° C) and the minimum 33° F (0.5° C). Slight ground frost occurs on average once a year. The temperature frequently reaches 80° F (26.6° C) in July, August and September, and it rises a few degrees above 70° F (21° C) on warm sunny days in May, June, September and October. During the rest of the year the minimum rarely falls below 40° F (4.4° C), and on sunny days a maximum of 60° F (15.5° C) can be expected. Gibraltar is about 15° F (8° C) warmer than London in winter and about 10° F (5.33° C) warmer in summer.

## WESTERLY AND EASTERLY WINDS

An interesting feature of the wind system at Gibraltar is the frequency of either westerly or easterly winds. Those from due east are slightly more frequent than those from due west, but the wind comes from one of these directions on more than half the days of the year. When winds from the south-west or north-west are added to those from due west and compared with a corresponding spectrum from the east, it can be said that the westerlies prevail. Winds from due north or due south are rare, but they cause the extremes of temperature. In summer a sirocco type of wind sometimes comes from the south, giving rise to temperatures of over 90° F (32° C), and in winter a katabatic type of wind from the mountains to the north can bring the temperature near to freezing point.

The frequency of due easterly and due westerly winds is partly caused by the funnelling effect of the Straits. Westerly winds are often associated with the Azores high-pressure system extending over North Africa, which brings fine weather; but wet weather with westerly winds is caused by Atlantic depressions or low pressures over the Gulf of Genoa. In summer low-pressure systems tend to develop over the mainland of Spain and over the Sahara. In late summer the Sahara low pressure often prevails, causing easterly winds. At times, however, there is a fine balance, and the forecasting of wind direction can be very difficult.

### THE LEVANTER

The east wind, which is known as the Levanter, has some special local features. It brings warm damp air off the Mediterranean, and this is forced upwards rapidly by the steep eastern face of the Rock, to cause cloud formation. Rain rarely falls, unless the easterly wind is associated with a depression, but the Levanter cloud is often a heavy one in late summer and humidities are frequently over 90 per cent in the town, where most of the effect is felt. In winter the cloud is much lighter, and the sun can be shining almost everywhere except in the town. Even in summer, when the cloud reaches out into the bay, there is sunshine on the eastern beaches. Here the cloud can be seen forming towards the top of the steep slopes to cast its shadow on the other side. The Levanter is a scapegoat for many things rather than a source of real discomfort or cause of any ill effects. Blaming the weather for various troubles is a British characteristic that has been exported to Gibraltar, and the Levanter is well suited for this role.

Local weather variations are accentuated by the Levanter, but they are present in most weather conditions. Windmill Hill, Europa Flats and the airport area are usually bright and breezy, so that the streets of the town sometimes seem damp and airless in contrast. On the eastern side the main features are morning sunshine and afternoon shade, the latter caused by the sun going behind the steep face of the Rock in the middle of the afternoon; it is a disadvantage in winter, but the sun stays longer in summer, and shade on the hottest afternoons can be a relief.

Before a runway was built on the isthmus, the only aircraft operating from Gibraltar were seaplanes, which took off and landed in the harbour. For them the Levanter could be a serious hazard, as it causes strong downward eddy currents on the western side of the Rock. Various experiments were carried out between the world wars after some accidents to aircraft, and it was found that currents with a speed of 25ft (7·6m) per second were quite common.

The large amount of moisture that hangs over the Rock in the Levanter cloud has led to thoughts of condensing some of it to supplement the rainfall. Early in the current century wire netting fixed to a frame was tried as a means of bringing about condensation, and more recently nylon netting has been tried. Both produced some water, but the idea does not seem to be an economic proposition.

### THE ECONOMICS OF CLIMATE

Rainfall to supply water was once Gibraltar's most important climatic consideration. The saving in costs when rainfall provides plenty of water has already been mentioned, for 1in (25·4mm) of rain on the eastern catchments yields 650,000 gallons (2,954·9hl) of water. The annual average rainfall of 31·9in (810mm) thus provides around 15 per cent of requirements. It is still a useful saving when there is a large rainfall in any year, but sunshine to attract visitors is a more important asset. During the months between May and the end of September a visitor interested in the sea and the sun can feel assured that he will not be disappointed. There may be wet days, but he can be certain of returning home with a good sun tan if he wishes. During the rest of the year some warmth and sunshine are nearly always to be found, and the cooler months are better for walking and looking at the many interesting things to be seen on the Rock.

### THE SEAS AROUND THE ROCK

Strong currents are a feature of the seas round about. There is a general flow of water from the Atlantic into the Mediterranean at the surface level, which provides replenishment for the Mediterranean waters lost by a high rate of evaporation. Except when a strong east wind is blowing, there is a westerly current of about 2 knots in the centre of the Straits. At levels below about 70 fathoms the flow is in the opposite direction at a slower rate, with more saline and heavier water going into the Atlantic.

The Atlantic water flowing into the Mediterranean keeps the seas cooler than they are in most places further east, most noticeably from the point of view of sea temperatures in the middle of summer. Between the months of May and November a 10-year average shows that the water temperature in the Bay of Gibraltar stays above 60° F (16·6° C) for the whole period. The average does not, however, rise above 66° F (19° C) for any one month. There are substantial variations from year to year, and warmer water can be found in enclosed areas near the land.

The seas in the Straits are frequently choppy but seldom rough. Although the anchorage in the Bay of Gibraltar is sometimes affected by south-westerly gales, the incidence is limited on average to about five days a year. Fog is sometimes a hazard, but generally sunny weather is a feature of the Straits, even when cloud collects around the coast. In the past this was an important feature for observation from the fortress, and now it is much appreciated by the many yachtsmen who sail around the coast in small craft.

There is not much commercial fishing from Gibraltar, but

there are plenty of fish. For sporting fishermen the area is interesting as a meeting point of Atlantic and Mediterranean waters. Plenty of mackerel are available on spring and summer evenings, and bonito, a larger fish of the same family, can be caught in winter. A blue shark weighing 202lb (91·63kg) has been caught far out at sea, and there is much competition over stone bass, one weighing 84lb (38·1kg) having been caught. Around the rocky coasts on the south-western side there is good fishing for bream, which can also be caught off the North Mole.

There is still some scope for the development of both sailing and fishing in the waters around the Rock and further afield. The weather is sunny, there are good sailing breezes and plenty of fish can be caught.

PLANT LIFE

Most of the surface of the Rock is inhospitable to plants. They have to live in shallow soils of a highly alkaline nature and to be able to survive drought. There is no frost to trouble them apart from very slight occasional ground frost, but otherwise there seem to be few advantages. It is, however, surprising how much plant life thrives.

There are three distinct zones for indigenous and naturalised species. Firstly, there is the Upper Rock largely covered with trees, shrubs and herbaceous plants. Secondly, there is the area around Europa Point, where the influence of salty sea air is very strong and only small shrubs and herbaceous plants have become naturalised. Thirdly, there are the sandy slopes on the eastern side, where once again some plants have become naturalised.

On the Upper Rock evergreen olive trees predominate, but there are some pines, among which the *Pinus sylvestris* is common, and eucalyptus trees have been planted in avenues along many of the roads. The olives are not of the fruit-bearing variety and they have no economic value. There are some interesting differences in their habit of growth. In most places on the Upper Rock they form small trees, but at the southern end, where the wind nearly always blows strongly from one direction or another, the olives adopt a more shrubby habit.

Beneath the olives there is a varied shrub growth, including the *Ruta aquitifolia* of the rue family; *Cytisus linifolius*, a broom; and *Calicotome villosa*, a widespread prickly shrub rather like gorse. A common climbing plant among the shrubs is *Smilax aspera*, which belongs to the lily family.

A small plant of much interest is the *Iberis Gibraltarica*, the Gibraltar candytuft. It is a native of North Africa, and Gibraltar is the only place on the European continent in which it grows naturally, flowering on the Upper Rock in March. Another common small plant in the same area is the *Alyssum maritimum*, the sweet alyssum, which grows among rocks and crevices and flowers in winter. Many bulbous and tuberous plants are well adapted to a dormant dry season; on the Upper Rock the *Narcissus tazetta* is a common example, with a flower composed of a number of small florets. It is often known as the paper white narcissus, and can be seen in flower in November and December before the first narcissi have appeared in florists' shops in Britain. Other common small plants on the Upper Rock are the asphodel, *Asphodelus microcarpus*, which flowers in February and March, and the rosy-flowered onion, *Allium roseum*, which is in bloom a little later.

There is a great risk of fire during the dry summer, and fire breaks have been cut on the Upper Rock. The danger has increased with the growth of the tourist industry, and great efforts are made to keep visitors to the Upper Rock aware of the danger.

In the Europa area the red-hot poker, *Aloe arborescens*, is much in evidence. It was originally planted in Governor's Cottage, now part of an army establishment off Europa Advance Road, and has become naturalised, together with a number of other plants. The silver ragwort, *Senecio cineraria*, with a leaf like a *Cinneraria maritima*, is one of these, and the *Alyssum maritimum* can be seen once again in rocky places. An interesting plant is the squirting cucumber,

*Ecballium elaterium*, whose inedible fruit, when ripe, resembles a cucumber and squirts a liquid when touched. The sea lavender, *Limonium spathulatum*, is also common in the area, but nothing of any large size flourishes. The poor soils, salt air and strong winds are too inhospitable for bigger growth.

In the Catalan Bay area on the eastern side of the Rock great effort has been necessary to get anything to grow on the sandy slopes. Landslides have been a hazard, so that establishing soil-binding plants has been important. A useful one is a mesembryanthemum now known as *Carpobrotus acinaciforme*, which is a drought-resistant succulent creeper. Two leguminous plants, the *Lotus creticus* and the broom *Cytisus linifolius*, have also become naturalised. A small tree of the tamarisk family, the *Tamarix gallica*, has become established in places on the slopes, and gives some good binding from roots that strike deeper than those of the leguminous plants.

The different zones of plant life in a small place such as Gibraltar provide more interest than might be expected. As well as the plants already mentioned, many well known British plants can also be found on the Rock, including bugloss, fennel, Spanish broom, lupin, catmint, valerian, foxglove, bell flower, spurge, ragwort and Traveller's joy.

## GARDENS

There is not much room on the Rock for public or private gardens, but fortunately the Alameda Gardens were laid out on some of the only fertile ground in 1816. The gardens have some affinity both to gardens in southern Spain, as a result of growing similar types of plant, and to English public gardens, with their paths, flower beds and areas for sitting. There is a miniature golf course, but there are no lawns as in English gardens, since grass will not thrive without watering during the summer, and the wells in the vicinity are too saline for this purpose.

The gardens are colourful at all seasons except at the end of summer and early autumn, but even then a few geraniums and other plants make some show. Rain soon brings the gardens into bloom again, and shrubs such as hibiscus, plumbago, lantana, datura and bougainvillea give a cheerful display. Later in the season many smaller plants, such as irises and asphodels, come into flower. There is some overhead shade in the gardens from cypress trees and a few pines, including the Aleppo pine; and some citrus trees blossom and give ornamental fruits. The hillside site of the gardens gives one the opportunity of taking a seat with a westward view over the harbour and the bay, and at times there are brilliantly coloured sunsets behind the hills west of Algeciras.

Other gardens worth mentioning although not open to the public, are those behind the Convent, the Governor's residence in Main Street, and at the Mount, the Admiral's residence. These, like the Alameda Gardens, support both tropical and temperate species of shrubs and plants.

In the town area and elsewhere there are many small gardens within the walls of Spanish-style patios, some of which provide pleasant areas in which to sit. The shrubs and plants common in the Alameda Gardens are also to be found in private gardens. Climbing shrubs, such as varieties of bougainvillea and lantana, are particularly suitable; and cacti are also grown, as they look after themselves during the dry summers. These small town gardens have often been well designed to give shade in summer and sunny corners in winter.

### ANIMAL LIFE

Fossil remains already mentioned show that large animals once lived on the Rock, but among mammalian species only rabbits and a few small rodents are known to remain in a completely wild state. Some naturalists think there may still be some foxes, but the imported Barbary apes are the most evident mammalian animals. The Moors brought them in the first place but they have been reinforced with fresh stock from North Africa, most notably during World War II, when Sir Winston Churchill ordered more apes to be brought as they were reported to be in danger of becoming extinct. There is an old Spanish superstition that the British will go when the apes leave the Rock, so the British Prime Minister was not taking any chances.

There are now about forty of the animals in two packs. Although known as apes they are really monkeys of the species *Macaca sylvana*. Until the first few years of the present century they lived in a wild state. At this time a member of the garrison was put in charge of them and they were taken on to the station strength to prevent the numbers declining. In 1915 they became the responsibility of a commissioned officer and the commanding officer of the Gibraltar Regiment is now in charge of their care. At times they have caused trouble by marauding in the town. Once they used to be blamed for almost anything that was lost, and they still tend to indulge in mischievous peculation. Warning notices near the Apes Den station on the cable car route up the Rock point out that wallets and cameras have been known to be taken by the animals.

BIRDS

The Barbary partridge has been described as more interesting than the Barbary ape, because of the puzzle of its only being found in Gibraltar outside its African habitat. The red-legged partridge, a cousin of the same species, lives in southern Spain, but the Barbary variety only dwells on the Rock, where there are no red-legged partridges. The Moors are thought to have brought the Barbary partridge, as it cannot fly such long distances as that across the Straits. If they were introduced by the Moors, however, it is perhaps surprising that they have remained naturalised in such a small area. It is not known whether earlier generations were better fliers, but now even flying across the isthmus without a staging post would be a long way for them, so introduction by the Moors is perhaps the most likely explanation of their presence. They are thought to be declining in numbers at present, which might be associated with the opening up of the Upper Rock to the public in recent years. Exclusively military areas are known to become nature sanctuaries. Whatever their history may be, the Barbary partridges give much scope for ornithological research.

As well as the Barbary partridge there are about fifteen resident nesting birds. Some, such as the peregrine falcon, are represented by only one or two pairs. Others include barn owls, little owls, wrens, warblers, blue rock thrushes, blackbirds, blue tits, serins (yellow finches) and herring gulls. The last are interesting in being the Mediterranean birds with yellow legs as opposed to the northern European members of the family with pink legs.

All the nesting birds can be seen in the Upper Rock area, but the town birds are also interesting. Blackbirds, being tree-dwellers, are comparatively rare, but blue rock thrushes take their place in some gardens with little rocky crannies. House sparrows, another common nesting species, tend, however, to predominate in town gardens to a degree not often seen elsewhere.

The migratory birds are of great interest, as Gibraltar lies on one of the three main routes out of Europe. The other two routes run across the Bosphorus and down through Italy. The Straits of Gibraltar are a useful short-sea crossing at the western end of the Mediterranean, particularly for many large birds of prey, as they cannot easily fly long distances over the sea. When flying over land in daytime they are helped by upward thermal currents, but these do not develop in the same way over the sea, so that the birds have to rely more on the power of their wings.

Some migration is going on during nearly every month of the year. At the beginning of autumn in September kites and large flocks of honey buzzards are on their way south. The latter are present in very great numbers around the Rock in some years, but there are fewer when the wind is persistently a Levanter, as this blows them towards the other end of the Straits. In summer the honey buzzard lives on the contents of bees' and wasps' nests, but during migration it lives on small mammals and small birds.

In October other birds of prey, such as booted eagles, marsh harriers and sparrow hawks, are migrating, together with such seabirds as gannets, black-headed gulls and terns. Many smaller birds are moving southwards in November, including various finches, linnets and siskins. For some species the Rock is a wintering area: there are generally some gannets to be seen during winter months and crag martins find themselves winter quarters on the Rock.

December and January are months with little migration, but in the area around Europa Point there is often something interesting to be seen. Weather variations from year to year make a difference, and northbound flights sometimes begin in January, though generally birds wait until the end of February. March, April and May are months of great activity. The large birds of prey, such as kites, eagles and kestrels, start the season, followed by flocks of smaller birds, including finches, wheatears and warblers. The honey buzzard appears again in April and swifts also go northwards during this month. Some remain for the summer, but most spend a little time further north in Spain and are on their way south again by the end of July.

The interesting features of bird life around Gibraltar lie partly in the number of species to be seen – over 200 have been identified – but perhaps more in the habits of the birds and the close relation of these to their capabilities, climatic conditions and variations in weather patterns. Wet weather brings many birds down on the Rock to await an improvement. West winds bring many more migratory birds than east winds. A spell of warm and sunny weather in the winter often induces early movements northwards. Although Gibraltar has few mammalian species, its position on a main migratory route for birds makes up for this from a naturalist's point of view.

# 3    *TARIK'S MOUNTAIN*

GIBRALTAR provided a suitable place for habitation when men were cave-dwellers and hunters, but as their needs became more sophisticated, requiring farm land and a readily available water supply, it suffered from neglect. Some writers, such as the Greek geographer Strabo and the Hispano-Roman Pomponius Mela, wrote about it, the latter describing St Michael's cave on Mons Calpe about AD 40 as an extraordinarily marvellous hollow with its opening half-way up facing west.

It was not until nearly seven centuries later that events in Africa and Spain brought the strategic position of Gibraltar to the forefront. Then, at the beginning of the eighth century, the Saracens under the Caliph Al Walid were in control of the western provinces of North Africa, though Ceuta still remained in the hands of Count Julian, who was at odds with the Visigoth kingdom in Spain. King Roderic was accepted as ruler by some of the Visigoths, but there were a number of factions among them. Count Julian is said by some historians to have had a personal feud with Roderic, who was alleged to have seduced Julian's daughter, but this may have been no more than an excuse on Julian's part for pursuing his own ambitions with the help of Musa ibn Nusayr, the subordinate ruler of the Caliph.

### MOORISH EXPEDITIONS

In 710 a reconnaissance expedition was fitted out and despatched across the Straits. The commander was Tarif ibn Malik Nakli and the expedition landed near Tarifa Point. Much ravaging and pillaging of the countryside was carried out by between 500 and 1,000 men and the force returned with plenty of spoil and some men and women slaves. Musa was thus persuaded that a full-scale invasion of Andalusia would be worth while, so plans were prepared to send an expedition of about 500 horsemen and 7,000 foot soldiers. Tarik ibn Zeyad, a freedman, was put in charge of this force. As a result of the similarity of his name to Tarif there has been some confusion at times over who was the commander in April 711 when the full-scale invasion of Andalusia began, but it is now well established that it was Tarik.

Most historians have stated quite definitely that Tarik landed on the mountain that subsequently bore the name Gebel Tarik, but recently some doubts have been cast upon this belief in *Rock of Contention* by George Hills, which contains some theories not previously put forward. It is clear from most historians that Tarik first attempted a landing at some point on the coast that was not the Rock of Gibraltar, but he met with opposition and withdrew. He returned to another landing point and put his men ashore without opposition. This second landing is generally regarded as being on the Red Sands near the present Alameda Gardens, and there are no very strong reasons for doubting this. It would have been possible to land unobserved on the uninhabited peninsula from the few ships used on a succession of nights. The opposing forces around the mouth of the Guadarranque and elsewhere on the shores of the bay would be unlikely to have observed such a landing from 5 miles (8km) away even on a clear moonlit night.

Establishing a base on a peninsula would also have been good tactics for a competent commander like Tarik. If the landing was discovered, there would have been good defensive positions for men armed with spears and long bows while more troops came ashore. George Hills thinks it more likely that, after failing at the first landing place, Tarik took his ships around Europa Point to Punta Mala, about 5 miles to the north on the Mediterranean coast. This area would have had advantages in providing a better water supply and also pasture, but there would not have been the good defensive positions available while more troops disembarked.

*Plate 1* From the south-east: the harbour is on the left and the water catchments are the white areas (*GTO*)

*Plate 2* The steep eastern faces of the Rock with the Caleta Palace Hotel in the centre (*GTO*)

Town and beach: *Plate 3 (above)* Main Street, the shopping centre (*GTO*);
*Plate 4 (below)* Camp Bay and its bathing and other recreation facilities (*GTO*)

The provision of adequate water for men and horses would have been the greatest difficulty at Gibraltar. During Moorish times wells were sunk on the Red Sands, but this would have been a formidable operation shortly after landing. There might have been plenty of rainfall, with the possibility of using surface water running off the Rock, but April is not a particularly rainy month in most seasons. The difficulty over obtaining adequate water does not by any means rule out Gibraltar as the landing point, but it must have been a problem that the commander had assessed and solved before arrival or one that he solved later.

There were only weak forces around the Bay of Gibraltar to oppose the Moorish invasion, so Tarik was able to advance inland rapidly. Roderic was up in the north dealing with a revolt amongst the Basques, but brought his forces south-wards as soon as he heard of the Moorish landing. Battle was joined in July in the plain of Xeres after a long march by Roderic's forces. His army was defeated and he was killed in the battle.

### THE FIRST MOORISH PERIOD

The period between 711 and 1309 can conveniently be described as the first Moorish period in Gibraltar. Tarik soon had virtually the whole of Andalusia under his control, so Gibraltar was no longer of much importance to him. Most writers say that he fortified the Rock, though there was no obvious reason for doing this. There were good communications between Spain and Africa through Algeciras and Tarifa, and any fighting with the Visigoths was likely to be far away. On the other hand, there were frequent dissensions amongst the Moors themselves, so Tarik might have thought it prudent to establish fortifications and a look-out point on the Rock. He incurred Musa's displeasure in 712 as a result of his great success, so perhaps he had some reason for setting up a strong point in the rear of his armies.

Whatever happened at Gibraltar during the eighth century, it can be said that nothing standing above the ground goes back as far as then. It is said that an inscription removed during the nineteenth century put the date of the first building in the area of the castle about 740, but there was probably an error in translation. Future excavations in the area may throw more light on this matter, if rebuilding in the town makes digging amongst foundations necessary.

By the middle of the eleventh century some Christian kings in Spain were acting together against the Muslim Moors, but rivalry continued between Aragon and Castile. In 1085 Alfonso VI of Castile captured Toledo. This and other successes brought Yusof ibn Taxfin to Europe in 1086 and he defeated Alfonso near Badajoz. Yusof's death in 1106 was followed by a period of further dissension among the Moors and more successes for the Christian kings. Alfonso VII of Castile captured Cordoba and reached Almeria in 1147, which spurred the Moors to action to restore the situation, and by 1158 they had recaptured most of the old Moorish kingdom.

In 1160 Al-Mu'mim ordered fortifications to be built at Gibraltar, to complement the fort already at Algeciras. There was to be a city known as Medinat-al-Fath, a city of victory, and the Rock was to be known as Djabal-al-Fath, meaning the mountain of victory. The plan for the city was apparently abandoned, and the new name for the Rock does not seem to have been adopted.

The Moorish Wall, which still exists as a ruin, dates from about this time and it is the oldest wall to be seen on the Rock. It runs for 500yd (457·2m) down the side of the Rock from near the summit, and it lies a little to the south of the present town. The wall was sited with a commanding view over the Red Sands, probably to protect the castle area from forces landing there and climbing up the Rock to outflank the castle area from above. In that area itself it is not possible to identify any part as dating from as long ago as the twelfth century.

During the 100 years after 1160 war continued between the Christian kings and the Moors, with success coming to the former when they abandoned their own intrigues and united against the common enemy. The Christian kingdoms began to deploy a navy against the Moorish kingdom of Granada, with its long coastline from Almeria to Cadiz, including fortresses at Gibraltar, Algeciras and Tarifa. In 292 Tarifa was taken from the Moors and in 1309 Algeciras was besieged. While this siege was in progress, Alonso Perez de Guzman was sent to attack Gibraltar, which he captured after a siege of one month. The inference to be drawn from the short duration of the siege, now known as the first siege, is that the garrison of 1,100 men were not fighting behind very strong fortifications.

### THE FIRST SPANISH PERIOD

After the capture of Gibraltar in 1309 the Spanish forces held it until 1333. The main objective in 1309 had been Algeciras, but when the winter set in with much rain, Ferdinand IV of Castile abandoned the idea of taking Algeciras, which was on one of the main supply routes for the Moorish forces. Ferdinand thought he could use Gibraltar instead to attack Moorish supply lines, and put Alonzo de Mendoza, a well trusted officer, in charge of the Rock.

Efforts were made to encourage people to settle at Gibraltar. Freedom from punishment for many crimes was granted to encourage them, and those to be excused punishment included any woman who had escaped from her husband. The town that was established lay probably in the area known as Villa Vieja, the Old Town, on the present site of Casemates Square. The Moors besieged Gibraltar in 1316, after Ismail, a fanatical Muslim, had overthrown his uncle, but the siege does not appear to have been carried out with any great skill or determination, and it was called off when a relieving naval force arrived.

The Spanish failure to take Algeciras from the Moors eventually led to their loss of Gibraltar in 1333. The Moors had been handicapped by quarrels among themselves, but in 1333 Abd'l Malik arrived from North Africa with a besieging force. The town was under the command of Vasco Perez, a competent soldier but one who had amassed private wealth at the expense of the defences. Two towers had been built since 1309, but the Moors were able to get ashore and besiege the garrison closely in the castle area. The defences held out for over four months, but starvation forced the Spanish to surrender. They had eaten even their leather shields before they did this. Vasco Perez, however, had secret food supplies with which he had maintained some Moorish captives in good health in the hope that they would bring him a large ransom; and when he surrendered on 17 June, he still had supplies of food in his private store.

The desperate situation at Gibraltar had been known for some time to Alfonso XI of Castile, but he did not arrive with his army until the Moors were in possession. He took up positions on the isthmus and landed troops on the Red Sands, but the lack of opposition to the landing led to carelessness and the attackers were killed further inland in small groups, since they did not wait for a strong force to disembark before they advanced. On the isthmus Alfonso found himself in trouble in his rear, owing to his troops' failure to establish good defensive positions through pursuing a small Moorish force across the Guadarranque. Persistent east winds were another problem in preventing support being given to the first attack in the Red Sands area. Eventually Alfonso's troops succeeded in attacking the castle area with battering rams, siege towers and catapults. A stalemate was reached and a truce was made under which Alfonso withdrew his forces without molestation by the Moors. Thus the fourth siege ended with the Moors in possession of Gibraltar. The military tactics had consisted of a frontal assault from the isthmus and outflanking by means of a landing on the Red Sands. Time would have been on Alfonso's side, as starvation would have played its part if the attack could have been maintained.

The weapons used during the fourth siege were remarkable for being so out of date. The battering rams and scaffolds were little changed from those used in Roman times. The longbows used were post-Roman but still old-fashioned weapons, less helpful to the attackers than the defenders, who also used the ancient weapon of burning pitch to set the wooden scaffolds on fire. Gunpowder had been known for about 100 years and cannon were coming into use by 1333, but it was another 100 years before they played any significant part at Gibraltar.

The second Moorish period in Gibraltar began with another of the innumerable Moorish intrigues. Mohammed of Granada, who had agreed upon the truce with Alfonso, was murdered near Gibraltar because he was said to have broken his religious faith by eating with Alfonso, a Christian, as he had done after the truce was arranged.

There was a period of truce until 1338, while Alfonso waged war on Portugal and the Moors quarrelled among themselves in Africa. At the southern end of Europe they held the twin fortresses at Algeciras and Gibraltar, but Tarifa was still in Spanish hands. By September 1340 Abu 'l Hassan had assembled around Tarifa an army that may have numbered 150,000 men. The Spanish naval commander, Jofre Tenorio, who had taken part in the 1333 siege of Gibraltar, had been defeated in battle at sea, and the stage seemed set for a Moorish success in the recapture of Tarifa. Alfonso had much smaller forces available to him, but he obtained some help from his late enemies, the Portuguese, and from other parts of Spain, and succeeded in hemming the Moorish forces in on several sides, with the Tarifa garrison between them and the sea. Both Abu 'l Hassan's forces from Africa and those of Yusof of Granada were engaged, and heavily defeated, by the Salado river. Better discipline in Alfonso's army might have resulted in a much more decisive victory, but the troops interested themselves in Hassan's harem and the booty in the Moorish camp, returning to Seville with jewellery and precious stones without any attempt at dislodging the Moors from Algeciras or Gibraltar.

Following a defeat of Hassan's naval forces in 1342, a favourable opportunity again came for an attack on Algeciras. Alfonso laid siege to it in August, and he eventually entered the city in March 1344. The siege was one of attrition, in which the besiegers endured two winters in the open as well as sallies from the garrison and 'red hot balls of iron' hurled at them from cannon. This was the first instance of these weapons being used in fighting in southern Spain. Another interesting feature of the siege of Algeciras was the presence of Christian forces from outside Spain, for war on the Moors had assumed the nature of a crusade. The Earls of Derby and Salisbury were among English peers who took part. While the siege was in progress, Alfonso took steps to guard his flank from attack by the garrison of Gibraltar, but he did not attempt action against Gibraltar at the same time. A 10-year truce was made in 1344, when Algeciras had surrendered.

The truce did not last for the agreed 10 years, and in 1349 Alfonso was again turning his attentions to Gibraltar, now the last remaining Moorish fortress on the Spanish side of the Straits. Since its recapture by the Moors in 1333, the defences of Gibraltar had been greatly strengthened. Some of the works in the castle area, including the keep (also known as the Tower of Homage), date from this period, although the tower itself may have been on the site of an older tower. The castle assumed the form of the Upper, Middle and Lower Castles described by Colonel Thomas James in *The History of the Herculean Straits*, the Upper Castle encompassing the keep, the Middle Castle half-way down towards the sea and the Lower Castle in the Casemates Square area next to the waterport.

There are few details of actual fighting during the fifth siege, begun in 1349. Alfonso set up a large camp in the area around Gibraltar and obtained the naval help of some galleys from the King of Aragon. Misfortune overtook Alfonso's camp in the form of an outbreak of plague – the Black Death, which had ravaged much of Europe. Alfonso refused all suggestions that the siege should be raised, but he himself caught the plague in March 1350 and died. This marked the end of the siege after some eight months, although Alfonso had planned to carry it on for much longer. Without his leadership there was no heart for continuing the fight. He commanded respect among his enemies as well as his own forces, and after his death Moorish troops went unarmed to his camp to pay their respects. His army was granted a safe conduct back to Seville, and this was rigidly observed by all Moorish forces.

Alfonso XI had carried on the war against the Moors with distinction. He was a good military tactician and his leadership was outstanding, for he lived among his troops and shared their dangers and hardships. He also succeeded in obtaining Christian support from outside his kingdom of Castile for the war against the Moors. One of his failures was not pressing home his victory at the Salado river, and when he died, the Rock was still in Moorish hands. He cannot be blamed for the final disaster of plague in his camp in 1350 during the fifth siege of Gibraltar, but he might have moved more quickly to its relief in 1333.

Alfonso did not manage his domestic affairs as skilfully as his military campaigns, and left two claimants to the throne. He was succeeded by his son Peter, the son of Queen Maria and the lawful heir, but he also had sons by his mistress, Leonor de Guzman, a lady of noble birth and great beauty. She was murdered after Peter came to the throne, and her son Henry rose against Peter, killing him in 1369. Mohammed V of Granada had received support from Peter in his Moorish intrigues, so he proceeded to attack the ruins of the fortress of Algeciras after Peter's death, and captured it in a few days. Thus much of Alfonso's success on the field of battle was set at naught by the domestic discord that he left behind. The Moors were again in possession of both Gibraltar and Algeciras, although the latter was only a ruin.

In 1374 Mohammed V acquired Gibraltar from the King of Fez, apparently as a result of some bargain between them. At the beginning of the fifteenth century there was a revolt within Gibraltar against the Granadian rulers, and Abu Said took charge of the Rock in 1410 on behalf of King Fayd of Fez. In 1411 Ahmed, the son of Yusof III of Granada, laid siege to the Rock. He received some help from inside and captured the tower of the castle after a short siege – the sixth.

The next attack on the Rock was made by Henry de Guzman, Count of Niebla, who was the owner of much land between Cadiz and Tarifa and had suffered considerably from Moorish raids. He was a gallant officer, but his conduct of the attack was badly prepared. He landed troops in 1436 on the Red Sands before a fortifying wall that had been built on the site of the present Line Wall, but the Moors were waiting, and attacked from above. The count had remained aboard his ships directing the cannon, which do not seem to have been very effective. He came to the rescue of his stranded troops, but he was drowned and the Moors hung his body from the walls of the city.

An attack was also made from the isthmus, but it made little headway and it was called off when the count was killed. He had been far too optimistic in thinking a landing could be made in the seventh siege in 1436 in the same way as had been done in 1333 by Alfonso's forces in the fourth siege.

### THE END OF MOORISH DOMINION

The end of the Moorish occupation of the Rock was less notable from a military point of view than many other incidents since the first occupation in 711. By 1462 the Granadian kingdom was in decline, with many dissensions within it. This was matched by quarrels at the court of Castile, but it happened that in August 1462 some of the garrison of Gibraltar had gone to Granada, and the weakened state of the defences was reported by a deserter to Alonso de Arcos, the military governor of Tarifa. He went at once to Gibraltar with about 250 men, and after capturing sentries and torturing them for information, decided to wait outside the walls for reinforcements. He sent a message to his feudal overlord, the third Count of Niebla, who was also first Duke of Medina Sidonia; and when forces arrived from Vejer Jimena and ships came from Tarifa, there was fierce fighting with heavy losses on both sides. The garrison repulsed the attacks, but negotiations for surrender began after horsemen and infantrymen had come from Jerez and 300 lancers had been brought by Rodrigo Ponce de Leon, the son of the Count of Arcos.

There was much disagreement among the Spanish leaders over how the negotiations should be conducted and to whom the town and castle should be surrendered. It was finally agreed to await the arrival of the Duke of Medina Sidonia in order to follow correct feudal protocol, but in the meantime Rodrigo seized the town on his own initiative. When the Duke arrived, it was agreed that they should both accept the surrender of the castle, together with the Count of Arcos; but the Moors began separate negotiations with the Duke before the Count of Arcos had arrived, and he accepted the surrender of the castle on 20 August. After a quarrel between the Duke and Rodrigo it was agreed that they should both enter the castle together. A further quarrel ensued over the touching of the Duke's standard by a Moor as a token of surrender, but both standards were eventually hoisted side by side. The Duke's men moved into the castle in substantial numbers and Rodrigo withdrew his standard lest it should appear subservient. When the Count of Arcos arrived, quarrelling with the Duke continued, but eventually the Duke was left in possession.

Credit for the capture of Gibraltar is generally given to Alonso, who made the first moves from Tarifa. He died in 1477 and is buried in Seville with an inscription attributing to him the recovery of Gibraltar, which occurred on St Bernard's Day, 1462. St Bernard still remains the patron saint.

The Moorish occupation of Gibraltar assumed great symbolic significance for Spain, partly because of the belief that not only did Tarik land on the Rock, but he established a fortress there. It seems more probable that the fortification was of a much later date, for, in addition to other evidence, there are the writings of the traveller Ibn Battuta, which date the keep of the castle to the period between the sieges of 1333 and 1349. Other Moorish fortifications also date from this time, and some were probably built early in the fifteenth century.

## GIBRALTAR

During the Moorish period there was a fortress on the Rock, but later in history the whole Rock itself beçame a fortress. The Moors used the bluff of land on which the Castle stands as a strong point to guard against attack from the isthmus along a narrow causeway not protected by the north face of the Rock. When a sea wall was added, the fortifications were well designed for the weapons in use at the time. The loss of Gibraltar by the Moors was the result of the weakened state of the garrison and perhaps low morale of the troops.

# 4    THE SPANISH ROCK

S PAIN was still far from being a unified kingdom when
Gibraltar was captured. The Duke of Medina, Juan
Alonso de Guzman, considered that he had a prescriptive
and possessory right to Gibraltar, but Henry IV of Castile
annexed it to his kingdom. The Duke of Medina gave up the
Rock under protest, but in 1466 he began the ninth siege.
The governor, Esteban de Villacreces, withdrew into the
Castle area, where he resisted behind the outer walls for
ten months and then within the keep for a final five months.
He surrendered in 1467 to Henry de Guzman, the Duke's son,
who succeeded his father a year later, and then made peace
with Henry IV of Castile. This confirmed possession of
Gibraltar and territorial jurisdiction over the hinterland in
the Dukes of Medina Sidonia.

The Moorish kingdom of Granada had by this time almost
ceased to be a power of any consequence in the area, but
a large-scale Moorish raid was carried out in 1477. The
abandoned and ruined fortress of Algeciras was occupied for
a short time, but the Moors were driven out with the help
of a Castilian naval squadron.

### GIBRALTAR UNDER THE SPANISH CROWN

The marriage in 1469 of Ferdinand of Aragon with Isabella
of Castile had the effect of uniting the two kingdoms and
leading to the formation of the Spanish nation. Isabella
succeeded to the throne of Castile in 1474 and Ferdinand to
the throne of Aragon in 1479. Isabella confirmed the title
of Marquis of Gibraltar on the Duke of Medina and he
supported her in the fight against the Moors, Granada being

45

captured with his help in 1492. The death of the Duke later in that year led to a reopening of the question of the over-lordship of Gibraltar. The new Duke, Juan Alonso de Guzman, resisted the idea of surrendering it to the Queen, and the matter was not pressed for a time; in 1501, however, he agreed to surrender Gibraltar to Isabella and in January 1502 it was placed under the governorship of Garcilasso de la Vega. A Royal Coat of Arms was granted to the city, which it still retains.

During the period of control by the Dukes of Medina there had been much economic development in Gibraltar and the area around it, for the Dukes were wealthy men and controlled wine-growing lands and tunny fisheries. A port and cooperage industry were developed at Gibraltar and ships from many countries traded there. After Isabella's death in 1504 the Duke of Medina resumed efforts to recover Gibraltar in 1506, carrying out a blockade, now known as the tenth siege, but it was a half-hearted affair and was abandoned without any serious fighting.

Isabella appointed Ferdinand by her will as regent for her daughter Joanna, and he exercised power until he died in 1516. By this time Joanna's son had succeeded to the title of Emperor Charles V of the Holy Roman Empire, and on Ferdinand's death he became Charles I of Spain. He realised the importance of Gibraltar early in his reign and ordered improvements to be made in its defences, but by 1540 there had been a decline in preparedness for attack. Turkish pirates took advantage of this and made a raid on the Rock. They landed on one of the small beaches near Europa Point, scaled the cliffs and pillaged the shrine of Our Lady of Europa before attacking the town. They took away hundreds of hostages when they re-embarked to carry out further raids, but were caught at sea by a Spanish squadron and most of the captives were saved.

The Turkish attack is not numbered among the sieges, but it showed that the defences were weak. Attacks by pirates all around the coasts in the area were common at the time, and Gibraltar became a base for ships operating against them.

The northern defences were strengthened and the Charles V Wall was built to protect the town from the south. Part of the wall formed a barrier at the southern end of the town and a later extension runs straight up the Rock for about 250yd (228·6m); it stands 400yd (365·76m) south of the old Moorish Wall and commands a much better field of fire. It was likewise designed to prevent an enemy traversing the upper slopes of the Rock. There were no further landings by pirates, but some were driven off in 1558. Many other points along the coast of southern Spain were easier to attack after Gibraltar's defences had been improved. Partly as a result of the danger from pirates a commercial decline occurred in Gibraltar after it passed to the Spanish Crown from the Dukes of Medina. There was little civilian settlement and convicts had to be brought in to work on the defences.

The commerce of the whole of Spain suffered in 1609 when Philip III decreed that all remaining Moors should be expelled. The Moorish dominion had been broken by the fall of Granada in 1492, but about half a million Moors had remained in Spain. They were closely associated with the commerce of the country, but the Church considered it necessary to expel the remnants of the Muslim world, along with Moroccan Jews.

Philip IV visited Gibraltar in 1624. He complained to the governor, Luis Bravo, that the Landport gate was too narrow for his carriage; Bravo replied that it was designed to keep out the enemy. However, the whole area was reconstructed, with new bastions and defensive ditches, soon after the visit, and a larger gate was built. Further work on the fortifications was ordered by Philip IV, and this included a substantial strengthening of the Line Wall defences on the western seaboard. A number of gun platforms were placed along the wall and a battery was sited to cover the harbour and the New Mole, which had been built at the south-east end of the present South Mole. A number of light defences were placed at the southern end of the Rock to deal with any small parties of pirates that might clamber ashore. The whole Rock was thus beginning to become a fortress, as opposed to simply accommodating a fortress, as it did in Moorish times.

By 1627 Gibraltar was one of the most strongly fortified places around the Spanish coast. There had been some threat to Spain from Charles I of England, but this petered out amid his own troubles with Parliament. Oliver Cromwell later considered the possible value of Gibraltar to Britain, but Spain was more seriously threatened by France, to whom much territory was ceded in the Pyrenees in the middle of the seventeenth century. Interest in Gibraltar tended to decline. There was a possible threat from English and Dutch sea power, but the fleets of both countries were received in Gibraltar from time to time.

In 1662 England acquired Tangier from Portugal as part of Catherine of Braganza's dowry on her marriage to Charles II. Tangier's position at the western end of the Straits made it better placed than Gibraltar as a naval base for the sea route around the Cape of Good Hope, but it was somewhat surprisingly abandoned in 1684, owing to the refusal of Parliament to provide funds for its maintenance. Part of the price of quarrels in England between Charles II and his Parliament was thus abandonment of a port that would have have been very useful a few years later. Its retention might have altered the history of Gibraltar.

After the death of Charles II in 1685 James II succeeded to the throne, but he had to abandon it to William of Orange and Mary in 1688. James II fled to France and he was supported by Louis XIV, who with the aid of the French army wielded great power in Europe. In 1689 Britain, Spain and the Netherlands joined Bavaria and other German states in the War of the League of Augsburg against France. James II was defeated at the battle of the Boyne in 1690, but the British and Dutch fleets suffered some defeats early in the war. There was a victory off La Hogue in 1692 in which Admiral Sir George Rooke distinguished himself, but a year later he was in difficulty when escorting 400 merchantmen to Smyrna and other Mediterranean ports; he was heavily outnumbered by a French fleet and had to disperse his convoy, which suffered severe losses. Some of the warships and merchantmen made their way to Gibraltar, which was bombarded by some French ships; fire ships were also floated into the harbour and did some damage. The New Mole had been designed to give some protection from the fire ship hazard. It also provided gun platforms for use against the French ships – an improvised defence by the crews of the British ships without which the rest of the merchant ships might have been lost. Nothing much had been done to the defences of Gibraltar since Philip IV had ordered their improvement 70 years earlier.

The war ended with the Peace of Ryswick in 1697. France gave up some Dutch forts and the parts of Catalonia she had obtained from Spain earlier in the century, and William of Orange was recognised as King of England; but a problem arose from the ailing state of Charles II of Spain who had no children. Britain felt threatened by the possibility of Philip V succeeding to the Spanish throne, for he was a grandson of Louis XIV and his succession could have led to Bourbon monarchs on both thrones uniting the kingdoms of France and Spain. The Partition Treaties of 1698 and 1700 were therefore designed to preclude Philip V from succeeding to the Spanish throne.

When Charles II of Spain died in 1700, Louis XIV recognised Philip V, contrary to the agreement in the Partition Treaties, but there was the authority of the will left by Charles II for the succession of Philip V. Britain supported the claims of the Archduke Charles of Austria, of the Hapsburg line. William of Orange wished to declare war, but Parliament delayed the matter; and the issue was eventually decided in favour of war when Louis XIV recognised the Old Pretender as James III, King of England, on the death of James II in exile in France. The War of the Spanish Succession began in May 1702 after the succession of Queen Anne in England, on the death of William of Orange. Britain was allied with the Netherlands and Austria against France, with the object of substituting Charles III on the throne of Spain for Philip V; there was no war with Spain as a nation, although fighting with the supporters of Philip V was inevitable.

In February 1704 Sir George Rooke took the Archduke Charles to Lisbon ahead of his main fleet. He had been instructed by Queen Anne to put himself under the command of the Archduke, who wanted a base from which to operate, so Rooke sailed to Barcelona as requested with troops under the command of Prince George of Hesse. An expected insurrection in favour of Charles III among the Catalonians did not occur, so the troops were withdrawn. After this unsuccessful action Rooke tried to find the French fleet, but he also failed in this at a time when a defeat of the French at sea would have been most welcome in Britain.

In July a council of war was held aboard Rooke's flagship, the *Royal Catherine,* off Tetuan, and it was decided to make an attack upon Gibraltar. The garrison was known to be weak and the defences were still in poor shape. A base was needed for use during the rest of the war, there was prestige value in having Gibraltar in the hands of Charles III, and Rooke himself was happy to have a chance to redeem an otherwise unsuccessful summer at sea.

According to British historians the attack on Gibraltar began on 21 July, but Spanish histories give the date as 1 August, since Spain had adopted the Gregorian calendar, but Britain had not yet done so. On the Gregorian calendar date of 1 August about fifty ships anchored in the Bay of Gibraltar on the western side of the Rock. About 2,000 marines were put ashore in the afternoon on the isthmus under the Prince of Hesse, who called upon the governor, Don Diego Salinas, to surrender, but received the reply that the people of Gibraltar had taken the oath of allegiance to Philip V. Salinas decided to defend, although he only had about 100 properly trained men and very few gunners to man his 120 guns, which were mostly very old weapons.

An east wind kept the fleet away from Gibraltar on 2 August, but on the next day it opened up with a very heavy

Gardens: *Plate 5 (above)* the Gibraltar Arms in the Alameda Gardens showing the key and the words 'Montis Insignia Calpe' spelt out *(GTO)*; *Plate 6 (below)* an upper Rock road lined with eucalyptus trees *(GTO)*

Occasions: *Plate 7 (above)* changing the guard at the Convent; *Plate 8 (below)* procession at Catalan Bay which ends in the Bishop blessing the water (*GC*)

bombardment after some warning shots. About 15,000 rounds were fired in 6 hours. The defenders of the New Mole were overcome by the bombardment, and Captain Hicks was able to land there with some sailors and marines. A magazine exploded under them and they suffered about 100 casualties in killed and wounded. The explosion may have been set off by the defenders, but it was probably accidental. A little later Captain Whittaker with between 200 and 300 men went ashore in the Rosia Bay area, where they soon captured a small bastion now known as Jumper's Bastion after one of the officers who landed on the New Mole. In the meantime the Prince of Hesse was attacking from the isthmus, and he again called upon Salinas to surrender. Fighting ceased over-night and Salinas eventually agreed to surrender on the morning of 4 August. Most of the townspeople had fled to Europa, but many women there were in the hands of British troops. There was considerable disorder among the landing forces, who had by this time occupied most of the Rock. At Europa there was some plundering of the shrine of Our Lady of Europa. Admiral Byng, who was in charge of the landing operations under Admiral Rooke, tried to prevent violence against civilians, but it undoubtedly occurred.

The articles of capitulation signed by the Prince of Hesse on 4 August provided for the garrison to be allowed to march out with baggage, provisions for six days, and three brass cannon with twelve rounds for each. Civilian inhabitants who wished to do so could remain with the same privileges as they had had under Charles II, but they were required to swear allegiance to Charles III, who was proclaimed as sovereign over the city.

Remaining in Gibraltar was not a very attractive proposition, for it was under an army of occupation and the inhabitants had seen plenty of signs of bad discipline. This was described in some detail by Juan Romero, the parish priest, who remained to look after the church of St Mary the Crowned. Most of the inhabitants decided to take refuge in other towns, many settling in San Roque, just over the border, where the documents concerning the city were taken.

Many of the refugees suffered very severely and some died on their journeys.

It is suggested by some writers that Rooke ordered the British flag to be hoisted and took possession of the Rock for Britain. There is, however, no doubt that at the time of its capture Gibraltar was taken in the name of Charles III of Spain. Whatever flags may have been hoisted at any stage, the British did not obtain title to Gibraltar by capture.

Rooke sailed again about two weeks later with fifty ships, with which he succeeded in engaging the French off Malaga in a fierce but indecisive battle in which both fleets suffered heavily. The British ships were hampered by a shortage of ammunition after the bombardment of Gibraltar. Admiral Sir Cloudesley Shovel later described how he took his ship to within pistol shot of the enemy before opening fire with his guns, in order to avoid wasting ammunition. The French fleet returned to Toulon after the battle and Rooke took his ships to Gibraltar to refit.

Rooke's fleet had been at sea for six months, so he returned with most of it to England, leaving a squadron under Sir John Leake in the area. The capture of Gibraltar and the action off Malaga marked the end of Rooke's seagoing career. During 1704 he had succeeded in obtaining a naval base that gave Charles III a foothold on the Spanish mainland, but he had failed to destroy the French fleet, perhaps partly because of the expenditure of so much ammunition on Gibraltar. His success received a lukewarm reception in England. He suffered by comparison with the Duke of Marlborough, who had won the great victory at Blenheim in the same year, and, furthermore, he was a Tory and the Whigs were in power. He died in 1708.

The recovery of Gibraltar by the forces of Philip V soon became a major objective. By October 1704 a force of about 7,000 Spanish and French troops had been collected, and nineteen French warships arrived off Gibraltar. On 26 October the troops on the isthmus, who had dug trenches, opened fire with cannon. On 10 November the main assault was begun when a party of 500 men scaled the eastern side of the Rock

by a path known to a goatherd, who led them. They reached
St Michael's cave unobserved and hid there for the night, and
in the morning formed up on Middle Hill (near where the
cable-car terminus now stands) and attacked the defenders
from this commanding position in their rear. There was a
fierce battle in which Prince Henry of Hesse, the brother of
the Dutch commander Prince George, was wounded; but
the attackers had to surrender when they ran out of ammunition and the expected reinforcements of 1,500 men coming
by the same route had not arrived. The plan had also
included a frontal assault from the north and an attack from
the sea, but the former did not materialise and the latter was
prevented by the arrival of Admiral Leake with twenty ships.
The six French ships in the Bay of Gibraltar suffered heavily,
only two escaping eastwards, and one of these being caught
later. Leake's ships provided some naval reinforcements and
some supplies, but the garrison was still short of men, less than
1,500 remaining in good health and fit for action.

In December badly needed supplies and reinforcements
arrived. Leake was not able to spend much time in the bay
with his ships, as he might have been caught in confined
waters, as he had previously caught the French ships. It was
necessary also in winter to avoid the danger of being driven
on shore by westerly gales. He had, therefore, to place his
ships in positions from which they could help the garrison,
if the French attacked, and also defend any supply ships that
might arrive from England.

### THE END OF THE SIEGE

The twelfth siege continued into 1705. In January the
isthmus became very wet, owing to heavy rains, and sallies by
the garrison added to the discomfort of the attackers. Philip
V replaced his own commander, Villadarias, in February with
a Frenchman, Marshal Tessé. A French fleet of eighteen ships
arrived later in the month, but left without taking offensive
action; and in March Leake caught five French ships in the
bay and destroyed or captured them all.

In April Tessé withdrew his forces from the isthmus. By this time the Gibraltar garrison had been brought up to a strength of 4,000 men, and nothing less than a well consolidated land and sea attack could have succeeded. There was much argument about who was to blame for the failure to recapture the Rock, but the main fault was lack of coordination, particularly when surprise had been achieved by means of the advance by the goatherd's path.

Gibraltar was occupied in 1704 in the name of Charles III of Spain. Even after the siege designed to recapture it in the name of Philip V had failed, Gibraltar was still Spanish, though controlled by an army of occupation. From a military point of view the war brought Britain many successes, particularly on land in Europe, but the main objective, to place Charles III on the throne of Spain instead of Philip V, had not been achieved. Charles had little popular support in Spain, so the idea had to be abandoned in spite of victories over the French on land. At sea the war was indecisive.

# 5        THE BRITISH ROCK

NEGOTIATIONS to end the war with France and Spain were begun in earnest in 1711, 1,000 years after Tarik had landed on the Rock. A Tory government had come to power in Britain, and it wanted to finish the war. As part of a bargain for making peace the idea of keeping Gibraltar for Britain had been considered since 1705. Some Tories favoured the plan, but the army and the navy were against it. The fortress of Gibraltar was easy to blockade and bombard from the land and there were navigational and tactical difficulties around it for the navy. Changes of wind from east to west or vice versa could occur almost without warning and upset calculations and plans.

From the French point of view, letting Britain have Gibraltar at Spain's expense was an attractive idea. Philip V did not oppose it as strongly as might have been expected, but this did not prevent the plan from being a heavy blow to Spanish pride. Isabella's instruction in her will that Gibraltar should be kept by the Spanish Crown for ever was still revered by many people.

## THE TREATY OF UTRECHT

Article X of the Treaty of Utrecht made in 1713 granted Gibraltar to Britain. The article has been the subject of much controversy in subsequent years and the English translation is quoted in Appendix 2. It clearly ceded the town, the castle, the port and the fortifications to the Crown of Great Britain. The land and buildings granted were 'to be held and enjoyed absolutely with all manner of rights for ever, without any exception or impediment whatsoever'.

There could hardly be a more unequivocal grant, but the next sentence reads: 'But that abuses and frauds may be avoided by importing any kind of goods, the Catholic King wills, and takes it to be understood, that the above-named propriety be yielded to Great Britain without any territorial jurisdiction, and without any open communication by land with the country round about.' The treaty goes on to say that the denial of open communication by land is designed to prevent 'fraudulent importations of goods'. Later in the article Britain agrees to prohibit Moors and Jews from residing in Gibraltar, and undertakes to give preference to Spain in the event of wishing to sell or alienate the town of Gibraltar. All these items in the article have been sources of trouble.

The inclusion of 'territorial jurisdiction' was apparently concerned with trading practices, and it may have been intended to refer to the larger area known as the Campo de Gibraltar, of which the town and fortress were a part. It may have been intended to exclude any form of jurisdiction over the isthmus outside the walls of the town and fortress. There was a custom in places at the time under which jurisdiction beyond a fortress extended to areas within a cannon-ball shot, though Britain was known to favour twice the range of a cannon.

There is room for much legal argument about Article X of the Treaty of Utrecht, but it is clear that Britain derives its title to everything south of the fortifications, as they existed in 1713, from the treaty. The whole of the isthmus became known as neutral ground, and the position there needs to be considered in the light of subsequent events. The penalty for allowing Moors or Jews to reside in Gibraltar was not stated, but it could hardly be said to rescind the grant without a specific clause to that effect.

### THE YEARS 1713–27

In Spanish minds the yielding of Gibraltar was only a temporary arrangement, whatever the treaty said. The Rock had been lost before and recovered. In Britain after George I came to the throne in 1714 both he and his Secretary of State, the Earl of Stanhope, seem to have been strongly in favour of giving up Gibraltar in return for concessions from Spain.

Under Louis XIV French military power had been supreme in Europe, but it was weakened by the War of the Spanish Succession, and Louis XIV died in 1715. In Spain the ministry of Alberoni under Philip V set to work in 1715 to improve Spanish military power. This led to the forming of an alliance between Britain, France and Holland. The alliance became a quadruple one in 1718 when the Archduke Charles of Austria, who had become Charles VI and Holy Roman Emperor, joined the alliance. The accession of Spain at this stage might have been an adequate concession for ceding Gibraltar, but by 1720 opinion in the British Parliament had hardened against any concessions to Philip V.

There was much diplomatic activity by the Earl of Stanhope in 1720, designed to pave the way for a restoration of Gibraltar to Spain. In 1721 two letters reached Philip V from George I. The first offered Gibraltar in exchange for some other territory – Florida was among those in mind at the time – but Philip V rejected this letter and a second was sent, offering, without mentioning an exchange, to take the first favourable opportunity to put the restoration of Gibraltar to Spain before Parliament for approval. In the Spanish view the letter was an offer to restore Gibraltar in return for a cessation of all hostilities started by Alberoni in Italy and a restoration of British trading rights. These matters were being considered at the time, but the British view was that the letter simply expressed a personal willingness by George I to put the matter before Parliament. In Spain the letter became known as King George's promise.

Theoretically George I had the right to restore Gibraltar under the royal prerogative in foreign affairs, which the Act of Settlement of 1701 had left intact; but in fact the Revolution of 1688 had fundamentally altered the position of the monarch. The King was now dependent upon Parliament for his position. As a Hanoverian, George I was only moderately secure against a Jacobite restoration, and his wish for good relations with Philip V largely arose from fear of the 'Catholic King' giving support to the Jacobites.

The Earl of Stanhope died in 1721 and he was succeeded as Secretary of State by Lord Townshend, who saw no favourable opportunity to put the restoration of Gibraltar before Parliament. Relations with Spain deteriorated, although William Stanhope, the ambassador in Madrid and the brother of the Secretary of State, worked hard for peaceful relations. There was a building up of Spanish forces around Gibraltar, and by 1726 war became inevitable when a secret treaty came to light. Charles VI of Austria had agreed to support the return of Gibraltar to Spain.

The years between 1713 and 1727 had a lasting effect on the relations between Britain and Spain. On the British side there was a king who favoured giving up Gibraltar, and he was suported by some leading statesmen; but Parliament was against it and Parliament was now the ruling force in Britain. This point was probably not properly understood in Spain, so that Britain was thought to be acting in bad faith.

### THE THIRTEENTH SIEGE

Spanish forces gathered around the isthmus at the end of 1726. There were only 1,500 men in the garrison at this time and the defences were not in very good repair. By the end of February 1727 Spanish forces had dug trenches quite close to the Rock, and they began digging under Willis's Battery, intending to lay a mine under it, but in this they were unsuccessful. A force of between 15,000 and 20,000 men was mustered in the area near the Rock under the Count de las Torres, and the British troops were reinforced by about 500 men under Colonel Kane from Minorca, which Spain had also ceded to Britain under the Treaty of Utrecht. Colonel Clayton arrived from England with more troops before the fighting began, but the numbers of troops on each side was not particularly important. The siege was a gunners' battle, and the guns and mortars, numbering a few less than 200 on each side, were fairly evenly matched. The British were in command of the sea around the Rock throughout the siege, and soon after hostilities began in February 1727, Admiral Wager brought enfilade fire to bear on the troops on the isthmus from the eastern side of the Rock.

In April more troops were brought in from England, and in May the governor, Lord Portmore, arrived back with some troops. Portmore had been governor for 15 years, but frequently an absentee one; it was customary at the time to have a deputy in charge. The troops arriving with him brought the garrison strength to nearly 5,500 men. The Spanish troops had suffered severely from sickness during the winter, but shortly after Lord Portmore's arrival they set up a heavy bombardment. This did much damage, particularly in the Villa Vieja area (Casemates Square), but after about ten days the guns began to wear themselves out and either blew up or drooped at their muzzles. When the Spanish gunners became demoralised by the failure of their equipment, the British gunners replied with a powerful bombardment – and the besiegers had not the advantage of being able to shelter behind stone bastions such as those on the Rock. In June a truce was made, and this marked the end of the siege, although at the time there was a possibility of further hostilities.

The Count de las Torres had reckoned that he would require 25,000 troops to capture the Rock, but the main causes of his failure were faulty equipment and inability to prevent reinforcements and supplies reaching the garrison by sea. Landing places for men and supplies around the New Mole and at Rosia Bay were well out of range of the guns on the isthmus, so that ships could come and go unmolested. The siege cost the garrison 360 casualties from all causes, including seventeen deserters, while the Spanish army suffered 1,500 casualties from causes other than sickness and about another 5,000 from sickness.

There were long negotiations before peace was made. The opening rounds took place in Madrid, where Elizabeth

Farnese, the second wife of Philip V, played a formidable part. Philip V was a sick man, and Elizabeth was strongly against leaving Britain in possession of Gibraltar. The Count de Rottembourg was sent from Paris as a mediator, and there were many discussions between him and Elizabeth, who was said to have given vent to her feelings with 'unfeminine impetuosity'. She hated the British and suggested the exchange of a captured British merchant ship, the *Prince Frederick*, for Gibraltar. In Britain in the meantime opinion in Parliament had strengthened against giving up Gibraltar on any grounds, the Rock having achieved a symbolic significance in the cause of Protestantism against Roman Catholicism, although the latter faith flourished in Gibraltar itself, where the Jewish religion was also freely tolerated in spite of the Treaty of Utrecht. The British Parliament, however, regarded the cosmopolitan town as a bastion of Protestantism.

In 1728 the negotiations to end the war were continued at Soissons, and by March 1729 it seemed that deadlock had been reached; but Elizabeth's attitude changed when it was agreed that her son Charles by her first marriage should have Parma and Tuscany, and on that basis she agreed to the drafting of a treaty. In November 1729 the Treaty of Seville was signed. Gibraltar was not mentioned but the Treaty of Utrecht was confirmed. The meaning of the words 'without territorial jurisdiction' contained in the Treaty of Utrecht had been raised during negotiations, when Britain claimed that Spanish troops should withdraw beyond the range of a cannon according to normal custom. The Spanish troops withdrew to 1,000yd (912·4m) from the north face of the Rock, but this was stated to be only as a gesture of goodwill.

### EIGHTEENTH-CENTURY WARS

The Treaty of Seville did not solve any of the problems concerning Gibraltar, but for half a century it was unmolested. In the meantime it played a small part in the War of the Austrian Succession and the Seven Years War. During the former war preparations were made for a siege in 1746, but no active operations were undertaken. Ferdinand VI, who had succeeded Philip V, wanted peace, and the Treaty of Aix-la-Chapelle in 1748 once again confirmed the terms of the Treaty of Utrecht.

In 1756 the Seven Years War spread to Europe from North America, where British and French forces were already fighting, and the French landed on Minorca and besieged Fort St Philip. This brought the Byng family into the history of Gibraltar again. The Admiral present at the capture of Gibraltar achieved more successes at sea later and became Lord Torrington. His son, John Byng, received rapid promotion and commanded a fleet sent to reinforce Minorca. When he arrived in Gibraltar in May 1756, the position in Minorca was that only Fort St Philip remained in British hands. There was a disagreement between General Fowke, the governor of Gibraltar, and Admiral Byng about the troops escorted by Byng's ships; Fowke thought he should keep them, and only allowed Byng to take the men required to bring his ships up to full complement.

When Byng arrived off Minorca, there was a brief indecisive action with the French fleet, which was superior in strength. He saw that the relief of Fort St Philip was impossible and decided to preserve his ships. This action probably saved Gibraltar from being the next objective for the French fleet, but Byng was recalled to Britain to face a court martial, which acquitted him of charges alleging cowardice, but convicted him of not having done his utmost against the enemy. This carried the death penalty, and George II did not exercise his prerogative of mercy. Subsequently Voltaire wrote his famous words about England: '*Dans ce pays-ci il est bon de tuer de temps en temps un amiral pour encourager les autres.*' Fowke was also recalled, but suffered the lesser penalty of first losing his command and then being dismissed from the service.

During the early years of the Seven Years War both Britain and France tried to foster friendship with Spain. After the loss of Minorca William Pitt the Elder (later Earl of

Chatham) thought it would be to Britain's advantage to offer the return of Gibraltar in exchange for help in recovering Minorca. He considered Minorca much more important in lying within 200 miles (321·9km) of the French base of Toulon. Sir Benjamin Keene, an ambassador of great experience in Madrid, conducted some unsuccessful negotiations in 1757 in which the return of Gibraltar was one of the proposals, but he died in 1758. Spain was briefly at war with Britain in 1762, but the Seven Years War soon ended with the Peace of Paris in 1763, which left the status of Gibraltar unchanged but returned Minorca to Britain. During the war Gibraltar was never attacked, but it played a small part as a victualling base for the navy.

### EIGHTEENTH-CENTURY LIFE ON THE ROCK

Some governors of Gibraltar, such as Lord Tyrawley, who was there in 1756, had a poor opinion of it as a fortress, but most governors seem to have been content to enjoy a pleasant and lucrative life. The old Franciscan Convent was turned into the governor's residence in 1728 and it has served as such until the present. The eighteenth-century governors had emoluments largely composed of perquisites, which included fees for various permits, and payments for the sinecure offices of head butcher and chief baker, among others. Governors also received large quantities of wine, brandy and gin, estimated at about 6,000 butts per annum. Flogging was the penalty for drunkenness, but it does not seem to have been a very strongly applied deterrent, as the life of the garrison appears to have been one of much revelry, with the result that in the *Gentleman's Magazine* of 1757 the place was described as being worse than Sodom and Gomorrah. Relations with the Spanish across the border seem to have been good except in time of political stress. In 1759 Admiral Boscawan left a dinner party in San Roque to take his ships to sea when the French had been sighted. Helped by a Levanter he caught up with five French ships near Logos, destroying two and capturing the rest.

The Roman Catholic religion was deprived of some of its

churches early in the British days, but it continued in the church of St Mary the Crowned, which had hardly been damaged during the sieges. Some of its valuable statues and sacred vessels, however, had been sent to San Roque. In the days of Colonel Thomas James, who wrote *The History of the Herculean Straits* partly from personal experience, it seems that the priests were attuned to the life of the town. James wrote: 'They live very well and will drink freely and enjoy the fair sex: and one for his too libidinous life was recalled to Spain in the year 1752.'

## THE YEARS 1763–79

For 10 years after the Peace of Paris there was no apparent threat to Gibraltar. Restiveness in the American colonies leading to the Declaration of Independence in 1776 did not seem to pose any immediate threat. France and Spain were, however, awaiting a favourable opportunity to attack Britain.

There had been some neglect of Gibraltar's defences since their repair after the siege of 1727, but two men contributed greatly to putting them in order and getting the garrison in a fit state to fight. They were Colonel William Green and General George Eliott. Colonel Green was wounded at Quebec and posted to Gibraltar in 1761; he was an engineer and a competent gunner. General Eliott was a highly professional soldier, who was appointed as governor in 1776.

Green's talents were not greatly used before 1769, when he was allowed to go to England to put forward plans for improving the defences. In 1772 he was allowed to form a Soldier Artificer Company, the forerunners of the Royal Engineers, and in 1773 work began on King's Bastion midway between the Old Mole and the New Mole. By 1776 there were 300 cannon and mortars along the Line Wall and 100 guns, including 54 brass ones, on the northern defences. The guns at the northern end of the Rock were all ranged on targets in the Spanish lines.

General Eliott, who was in his sixtieth year when he arrived in Gibraltar in 1777, was a Scot educated in Edinburgh and at the University of Leyden in Holland. He spoke French and German fluently, had studied at the French Royal Engineer Academy, and had served in the Prussian army as well as the British army. In the latter he began as an infantry officer, but in 1759 he raised his own cavalry regiment. He was an austere man of great self-discipline, who had distinguished himself in the Seven Years War. He tried hard to prevent the common custom of indiscriminate plunder.

When Eliott arrived, much of the work on the gun emplacements had been done, but there was a need for men and equipment. By June 1779 the strength of the garrison was nearly 5,500 men, including three Hanoverian regiments. Eliott was still maintaining good relations with the neighbouring Spanish commanders, and on 19 June he went with some senior officers to congratulate General Mendoza on a promotion. He was received somewhat coldly, as Mendoza had heard of the proposed break between Britain and Spain, but it was not until Eliott returned to Gibraltar that Logie, the British Consul in Tangier, brought him similar news. The frontier was closed on 21 June and all members of the garrison and their families residing in Spain were sent back. Mendoza left to take up a new post soon after communications were cut.

### THE GREAT SIEGE

At the beginning of the fourteenth siege in 1779 the Spanish navy controlled the area around Gibraltar, and was able to impose a blockade. This weapon was the most effective one against the Rock's formidable defences. An attack from the north could only be made across a narrow causeway leading to Landport Gate, which still stands just north of Casemates Square. Between the causeway and the Rock there was an inundation, where the Laguna housing estate has now been built, and a narrow path led between the inundation and the Rock, but it was hardly a practicable line of assault. The guns of the Grand Battery west of Landport Gate covered the causeway from the south, and on the flank the guns of King's Lines and Queen's Lines were placed to fire across the inundation. About 70ft (21·34m) above these lay Prince's Lines, from which fire could be directed on to the isthmus. Still higher up, on the bluff of land running north-east from Moorish Castle, stood Queen Charlotte's Battery, Catalan Battery and Princess Caroline's Battery in an area known as Willis's Lines. These were the highest batteries at the beginning of the siege, but soon after the siege began a gun was hauled up 1,300ft (396·24m) to the highest point on the northern face of the Rock. This became known as Rock Gun.

Ships approaching the Rock could be engaged from whatever direction they might come, except on the eastern side. The west side of the isthmus was covered by the guns on the Old Mole, which became known as Devil's Tongue; and the direct approach from the bay was covered by a series of bastions along the Line Wall, extending from Montague Bastion near the Old Mole to the New Mole. From there southwards and around Europa Point a number of smaller batteries were placed to cover all practicable approaches. The eastern beaches might have afforded a landing ground, but there would not have been any line of advance from them, as the goatherd's path used in the twelfth siege in 1704 had been obliterated soon after that siege.

Following nearly three months of frustrating inactivity and an increasing blockade, General Eliott decided in September 1779 that it was time to open fire. The first shot was fired by the wife of a member of the garrison on 12 September on General Eliott's order 'Britons strike home'. Firing was carried on for a few hours from Willis's Lines and from Green's Lodge, a battery a little higher up the Rock set up after the siege had begun. There was not much return fire, but precautions had been taken in digging up paving stones in the town to lessen the effect of bursting shells. The main object of General Eliott's bombardment was to interfere with work on the Spanish lines, which ran from Fort St Philip on the western coast of the isthmus due east to Fort St Barbara on the Mediterranean coast, and lay about 1 mile (1·61km) from the north face of the Rock.

The opening bombardment brought to light a gunnery

problem. In earlier sieges much of the ammunition used had been solid shot, but more explosive shells were in use by 1779, and it was found that, when they exploded on the sand of the isthmus, the shells did little damage. Captain Mercier, an infantryman, solved the problem with the suggestion that shorter fuses should be used to produce air bursts. It happened that one of the garrison's officers during the siege was Lieutenant Shrapnel, who later designed the ammunition called after him, but Captain Mercier may have helped to set Shrapnel's mind in that direction.

By the end of 1779 the garrison was very short of food – a few ships from North Africa had managed to run the blockade, but not enough to supply 5,500 troops and 2,000 civilians – and an outbreak of smallpox in November was an added problem. In January 1780 a relief convoy arrived under Admiral Rodney, whose squadron, bound for the West Indies, was acting as escort to merchant ships bound for Gibraltar. He avoided the French fleet off Brest, but defeated a Spanish naval force off Cape St Vincent in a fight in which prizes were taken and Admiral Juan de Langara was wounded and captured. While a prisoner of war in Gibraltar, he was surprised to find that Prince William, the son of George III and later King William IV, was serving as a midshipman. He said: 'Well does Great Britain merit the empire of the sea when the humblest stations in her navy are supported by Princes of the Blood.'

Admiral Langara was returned to Spain under an exchange of prisoners of war, and the Spanish blockade was resumed by Admiral Barcelo after Rodney's departure with most of his ships. This blockade continued throughout 1780, which was a year of little military activity. The garrison was still subsisting on the supplies brought in by Rodney's ships, though scurvy was a troublesome disease and great efforts were made to grow vegetables to combat it. At the end of the year the Emperor of Morocco decided to give open support to Spain, which stopped a source of occasional supplies of fresh foods that evaded the blockade. There was an attack by fire ships in June, but the south-west wind dropped and helped the navy and the gunners to dispose of the ships without damage to British vessels in the harbour.

Diplomatic activity during 1780 was directed towards making peace, but Charles III of Spain, who had succeeded Ferdinand VI in 1759, tenaciously held to his ambition to retrieve Gibraltar for Spain. By the spring of 1781 supplies were again running short in Gibraltar, so Spanish hopes of capturing it without much fighting were revived.

In April 1781 a convoy arrived under the escort of Admiral Darby. There was no interference from the Spanish navy, but when the ships arrived, the forces on the isthmus set up a heavy bombardment. The ships unloading in the area around the New Mole and Rosia Bay were out of range but the damage done to houses in the town revealed hidden food and liquor supplies held by civilians. This led to looting by the troops, and the threat of very heavy penalties from General Eliott was needed to restore order. He himself did not drink spirituous liquor, and during the siege he had proved he could live for a week on 4oz (113.4gm) of rice a day. Prices of food had become very high before the arrival of Darby's ships. A wife of a member of the garrison wrote that 'very bad brown sugar cost half a crown a pound' and 'the worst tea that ever was used' cost 16s a pound.

The Spanish bombardment continued over a period of nearly two months, 75,000 shots and shells being fired. The 100 guns firing from the isthmus were supplemented from time to time by bombardment from the sea. After about six weeks the fire began to slacken, as some of the guns were developing droop in their muzzles.

Apart from occasional bombardments from the sea, the late summer and early autumn of 1781 were periods of inactivity. On the isthmus Spanish forces were advancing their works, posing a problem for the gunners high up on the Rock until Lieutenant Koehler designed a gun carriage from which it was possible to fire at an angle of depression. A model of his ingenious design can be seen in the Gibraltar Museum. In some respects it was the forerunner of much later recoil systems.

General Eliott and General Boyd, his second-in-command, made a careful study of the Spanish advanced works and noticed that there was some carelessness in defending them. A sortie was therefore carefully planned, and at 3am on 27 November, just as the moon was setting, about 2,000 men of the garrison moved out on to the isthmus under General Ross. They achieved complete surprise and destroyed most of the Spanish works. The Great Sortie was a military risk in using about one-third of the Rock's garrison, but the code word 'Steady' set the operation in motion exactly as it was designed. The arrival of Eliott himself at the front line was not in the plan, and he has been criticised for not leaving the operation to Ross; but Eliott had not the temperament to watch from a distance.

### THE LAST YEAR OF SIEGE

The blockade was not very strongly enforced for a time after Admiral Darby's arrival. He had left two gunboats behind under Captain Curtis, and these helped some ships through the blockade. By the end of 1781 it had became more severe again, and it was the main activity on the Spanish side after the Great Sortie. In March 1782 Minorca fell to Spanish forces, and this led to greater attention being directed to capturing Gibraltar.

Rewards were offered for plans to take the Rock, and many were submitted. The one adopted, the Chevalier d'Arcon's, consisted of an assault by land and sea preceded by a very heavy bombardment. For the attack from the sea old ships were fitted out with layers of timber interspersed with wet sand and wet cork so that they would not splinter. An attempt was made to counter the problem of fire arising from the use of red-hot shot by a system of pipes carrying water from overhead tanks to all parts of the ships. It was almost an early version of a sprinkler system.

Preparations for the attack went ahead throughout the summer of 1782, and on 13 September the attack was launched by ten of the specially designed floating batteries, each carrying between eight and twenty guns. They began bombarding the Rock at 10am from 1,000yd (914.4m) off shore. The land attack was opened with 246 guns from batteries across the isthmus. Against this there were only ninety-six serviceable guns on the Rock, but the gunners had put in some practice a week earlier with red-hot shot. This seemed ineffective for a time against the floating batteries, but early in the afternoon Admiral Moreno's ship started burning, to be followed by fires on other ships. By nightfall the bombardment from the sea was nearly over, and the bay was lit by burning ships. The next morning Captain Curtis was ready with his gunboats to harass the Spanish fleet, but he became engaged in rescuing survivors from the bay. During the battle Eliott characteristically commanded operations from King's Bastion at the centre of defences against the seaborne attack. Much publicity had been given in Spain to the attack on the Rock, and many spectators watched it from hills around the bay.

In October 1782 the third large relieving fleet came to Gibraltar under Lord Howe. There was nearly a disaster through a strong west wind taking many of the merchant ships past the Rock towards the Spanish and French fleets, but a change of wind to a Levanter saved the situation and Howe was only engaged in a minor action north-east of Ceuta. The arrival of fresh supplies following the failure of the assault in September initially marked the end of the siege, although hostilities were not suspended until 3 February 1783. The fourteenth is by far the longest and best documented of all the sieges. Captain John Drinkwater's *A History of the Late Siege of Gibraltar*, published in 1785, is a most authoritative work, for he served in Gibraltar throughout the siege in the 72nd Regiment.

The siege showed that the Rock could be defended by between 5,500 and 7,000 men in solidly built fortifications against the fire power that could be concentrated on it. Blockade was the most effective weapon, but General Eliott's leadership had played a great part in maintaining morale when starvation seemed almost inevitable. Against the Rock Spanish and French forces reached a maximum of over 40,000, but numbers were not of great consequence, as they could not be effectively deployed. The fighting was nearly all between gunners, as in 1727.

After the siege was over, the Duc de Crillon, the commander of the Spanish and French forces, was taken to see the defences of Gibraltar, including the galleries begun during the last year of the siege. The idea of tunnelling in the Rock was put forward by Sergeant Ince as a means of getting a gun to a point known as the Notch, from where it would have been possible to fire on to the Mediterranean shore near the north face of the Rock. The Notch was never reached in the tunnelling that continued after the siege, but the part of the galleries now called St George's Hall lies just below the Notch. Ince's tunnellers worked very hard with the equipment available and drove an 8ft (2·44m) square tunnel 82ft (25m) in five weeks. When tunnelling, it was found that there was a need for air, so holes were made in the side of the Rock. This led to the realisation that the holes would make excellent gun emplacements; by the end of the siege four guns had been mounted, but the work continued later to St George's Hall.

Preparations for the Great Siege and the siege itself gave rise to much ingenuity in Gibraltar, and Eliott encouraged this. Although a disciplinarian, he did not regard himself as having a monopoly of ideas. Not all the ideas put forward before or during the siege were good ones, and one piece of folly can still be seen in Healy's Mortar, which was carved out of stone on the Upper Rock near Charles V Wall and was designed to scatter stones on landing parties. It required a charge of 27lb (12·25kg) of powder, so it was an uneconomic weapon. It would in any event have been as dangerous to defenders as to landing parties.

POLITICAL EFFECTS OF THE SIEGE

The defence of Gibraltar was one success for Britain in the American War of Independence, during which she suffered many defeats. The idea of giving up Gibraltar in exchange for anywhere else was therefore not a feasible proposition for the British Parliament, though it would have contributed greatly to better relations with Spain. Charles III had been thwarted in his ambition, and in deference to Spanish pride there was no mention of Gibraltar in the Treaty of Versailles of 1783, which yielded Minorca and Florida to Spain. Britain once again had to be content with confirmation of the Treaty of Utrecht made in 1713.

General Eliott was awarded a CBE after the end of the siege, but it was felt in Britain that this was an inadequate reward, and he was raised to the peerage in 1787 as Baron Heathfield. There is a monument to him in the Alameda Gardens, and other soldiers are commemorated in various places. General Boyd, who later became governor, was buried under King's Bastion, and Sergeant Ince had a piece of land given to him called Ince's Farm, which still exists on the Upper Rock.

### THE NAPOLEONIC WARS

In 1788 Charles III was succeeded by Charles IV, and in 1793 Britain and Spain were associated in war against France, where the Revolution had begun in 1789. The Spanish forces were badly led by Godoy and Spain made peace with France in 1796. There was an agreement that France would help Spain to recover Gibraltar, but in 1797 Admiral Jervis inflicted a heavy defeat on the Spanish fleet off Cape St Vincent. Minorca was again taken by Britain in 1798, but it was handed back to Spain in 1802 under the Peace of Amiens.

There were two naval actions off Algeciras in 1801. Admiral Saumarez, unlike some of his predecessors, risked an action in the confined waters of the Bay of Gibraltar, taking six ships from Gibraltar in July to engage three French ships sheltering under the guns of Algeciras. He lost one ship and suffered damage to others, but he returned to the attack a few days later when two large Spanish vessels, the *Hermene-gildo* and the *Real Carlos*, came to escort the damaged French ships to Cadiz. In a night action the British ship *Superb* got in between the *Hermenegildo* and the *Real Carlos*, which fired at each other instead of the *Superb*, and both blew up with the loss of 1,800 men.

While British sea power was keeping Gibraltar free from attack, the state of the garrison was deteriorating. When Eliott returned to England in 1787, General Boyd had taken over, and he formally succeeded as governor in 1790 at the age of 80 years, when Eliott (then Lord Heathfield) died. Boyd died in 1794 and O'Hara succeeded him. O'Hara had served in a number of capacities since 1784 and had been lieutenant-governor from 1790 onwards. As governor he received an income of about £7,000 per annum from the licensing of some ninety taverns, in which many of the garrison of 7,000 spent much of their time. O'Hara entertained lavishly and was very popular with officers, soldiers and their wives. His nickname was 'The Old Cock of the Rock'.

By 1801 reports were reaching Britain about the poor discipline of the garrison, and O'Hara was succeeded by the Duke of Kent in 1802. He was the younger brother of the two sons of George III who became George IV and William IV, and was the father of Queen Victoria. The Duke of Kent, with instructions to restore discipline, closed many of the taverns and established a brewery on Europa Flats to provide beer to replace various imported spirits. In December 1803 first the Fusiliers and then the Scottish Borderers mutinied. The Dorsets remained loyal and the mutinies were settled after a number of death sentences had been carried out on the Red Sands, but the Duke was recalled and his request for a court of enquiry was refused. He remained as nominal governor until his death in 1820, but did not return to the Rock.

While in Gibraltar the Duke of Kent established very good relations with General Castanos, the Spanish commander at San Roque. Spain again joined an alliance with France in 1804, but unofficial contacts with the Spanish commander continued. A more serious trouble for the garrison in 1804 was a yellow fever epidemic, which caused the death of over 1,000 of the garrison and many more civilians.

In May 1805 Nelson's fleet visited Gibraltar, and in

October it came into Rosia Bay a few days after the battle of Trafalgar. Nelson's body, which was on board his flagship, was embalmed in wine and sent to Britain. Others killed in the battle were buried at sea, but some who died in Gibraltar of wounds were buried in the Trafalgar Cemetery, just outside Southport Gates. Most of the graves in this cemetery are those of members of the garrison and their families, some of whom died in the epidemic of 1804.

Nelson's victory at Trafalgar removed the possibility of Gibraltar being blockaded from the sea, as it had been at the time of the Great Siege. The port was developing commercially owing to Napoleon's Continental System, which excluded British ships from many ports, so that there was much transhipment of cargoes at Gibraltar into ships not excluded from other European ports. The good relations across the frontier with General Castanos were continued by Sir Hew Dalrymple, who took command of the garrison in 1806. Castanos was ordered to cut communications in 1807, but this was not made effective. In 1808 Spain again became allied with Britain as a result of a popular rising against the French, so that Castanos and Dalrymple became officially friends once again. When Castanos gathered his forces to fight the French, Dalrymple arranged for Spaniards from Gibraltar to join them.

In 1810 French armies reached San Roque. The inhabitants took refuge in Gibraltar, thus returning temporarily to the place some of their ancestors had left over 100 years earlier. The British commander in Gibraltar, General Colin Campbell. destroyed the Spanish forts of St Philip and St Barbara at the north end of the isthmus to prevent the French from using them, but there was no attack on Gibraltar.

In 1811 a force from Gibraltar was sent to relieve Tarifa, which was besieged by French troops, but at the beginning of 1812 the French withdrew from Tarifa and gradually left the whole area around Gibraltar. They were coming under pressure from Wellington's armies, and they had lost the sea power necessary to sustain offensive action in southern Spain. Gibraltar had become not only a fortress but also a supply base for the armies in Spain, a centre of entrepôt trade and a base from which naval forces and seaborne troops could operate around the coasts.

Lieutenant-General Sir George Don was appointed lieutenant-governor in 1814, but he is often referred to as the governor in relation to events between 1814, when he took up office, and 1832, when he died in Gibraltar. The Earl of Chatham succeeded the Duke of Kent as titular governor in 1820, but George Don was the man in charge in Gibraltar between 1814 and 1832. When he arrived, he appreciated the need for a civil administration, as there was a civilian population of 10,136, which would have been greater without the yellow fever epidemics of 1804 and 1813, as well as measures to restrict residence in Gibraltar. The second epidemic was still in progress when Don arrived. Little was known about the mosquito-borne disease, but it seemed to flourish in over-crowded conditions; persons who recovered had also been observed not to get the disease again. General Don obtained the agreement of General Alos, the local Spanish governor, to settle on the isthmus any persons who had not previously suffered from the disease. British use of the isthmus was as a matter of courtesy the subject of consultation at the time and the term 'neutral ground' was loosely used for the whole of the isthmus. A British watchtower called Devil's Tower had been established during the previous century 200yd (182.88m) north of the Rock and about the same distance inland from the Mediterranean coast, and the isthmus had also been used as a burial ground since 1756. Throughout Don's time good relations with the local Spanish authorities continued.

The end of the Napoleonic Wars in 1815 removed the need for the use of Gibraltar as an entrepôt port, but it continued to flourish as such for about another 15 years. By 1828 the civilian population was rapidly rising to 17,000, but another yellow fever epidemic came at the end of the year, causing

Plate 9 (above) A concert at St Michael's Cave (GTO); Plates 10 and 11 (below) a crag martin on the left and a honey buzzard (Charles Perez)

*Plate 12 (above)* The Home and Mediterranean Fleets congregate in the harbour in 1939 (*The Times*)

Old and new: *Plate 13 (left)* an old cannon points across the airfield and the isthmus into Spain *(GTO)* and *Plate 14 (right)* a Spanish water vendor in the 1930s

Hotels: *Plate 15 (above)* the Bristol Hotel, in the town right against the background of the Rock, overlooking the harbour *(GTO)*; *Plate 16 (below)* the Caleta Palace Hotel is in the background of this popular sandy beach *(GTO)*

1,667 deaths. The rapid growth of civil population and epidemics caused Don some formidable problems, but there are many monuments to his work, including the Alameda Gardens, the Law Courts, the Exchange Building and the Civil Hospital (now known as St Bernard's Hospital). There have, of course, been changes, and in the case of the hospital substantial additions. George Don was a governor liked by Gibraltarians, who first began to acquire an identity and to receive attention from a military authority. Money for the various works carried out was raised by lotteries, which were both popular and successful.

By the time Don died in 1832 the entrepôt trade was beginning to decline owing to steam vessels carrying cargoes direct to their destinations. The *Royal George* was the first steam vessel to call at Gibraltar, in 1823. Don's achievements in civil affairs included a Charter of Justice in 1830, and he left Gibraltar better able to cope with its civil problems. He was buried in the Cathedral of the Holy Trinity, which was built during his period of office.

### THE NEXT 60 YEARS

The next 60 years were quiet compared with those of the Napoleonic Wars and their aftermath, or with the sieges of the previous century. Gibraltar adapted itself to steamships by becoming a coaling station, although there was a decline in the use of the port. The opening of the Suez Canal in 1869 led to a gradual increase again in the ships using the port, but commercially the biggest development was the growth of a smuggling trade into Spain. A customs post was established at the northern end of the isthmus during Don's administration, but it was ineffective.

Tobacco was one of the most lucrative products for smuggling into Spain, but textiles from Lancashire also played a part. When Sir Robert Gardiner became governor in 1848, he tried to bring the trade under control, but this was very unpopular with the Exchange Committee, which met in the building established in the time of General

81

Don, who had encouraged such institutions. The Exchange Committee had powerful supporters in Britain, particularly in the Lancashire cotton industry, and Gardiner was replaced as governor in 1855. He did not give up easily, writing a long memorandum to Lord Palmerston after he had retired, and strongly criticising the colonial style of government set up by Don. In Gardiner's view Gibraltar should have been administered simply as a fortress. He saw nothing wrong with the governor presiding over criminal courts with the aid of a judge advocate, and called the supreme court set up in 1830 'an imitative empty pageant of the ceremonies of our high legal courts, full of sound and words, indeed, but of no usefulness in the cases of petty crime peculiar to the place'. Gardiner was a soldier who envisaged problems arising from having a large civilian population in a fortress, and hoped that stopping the lucrative smuggling trade and administering the Rock as a fortress would cause some of the civilian population to leave. Gardiner also foresaw problems arising in relations with Spain as a result of smuggling, with a consequent reaction against the fortress. Nothing happened as a result of Gardiner's representations.

Gibraltar suffered from a number of cholera epidemics, including a serious one in 1865 in which 420 civilians and ninety-eight members of the garrison died. This led to the establishment of Sanitary Commissioners, who were active for the next 50 years. This step was the first move towards Gibraltarian participation in government activities, though the Commissioners were appointed and not therefore representative of the people. A more representative role was fulfilled by the Exchange Committee, although Gardiner's trenchant pen described them as 'self-constituted and self-elected'. They sent a memorial to the Secretary of State in 1873 asking that the inhabitants should be allowed to peruse and consider local enactments before they became law, but they were told that this procedure would be 'inconvenient'. Five years later they achieved more success when the Secretary of State agreed to accept suggestions regarding a proposed customs scheme affecting the port.

After French troops left Spain at the end of the Napoleonic Wars, the Gibraltar garrison had a peace-time role for 100 years. Artillery weapons developed apace during the nineteenth century, and by 1880 guns with ranges of over 12 miles (19.31 km) had been devised. This led to arguments in favour of exchanging Gibraltar for Ceuta, which was enclosed by higher mountains, was roomier, and had a good natural harbour suitable for a naval base. Problems would have arisen over both the Gibraltarian population and the Spanish population around Ceuta, though politically such an exchange might have been acceptable in Spain, where the British possession of Gibraltar remained damaging to Spanish pride. Nothing happened, however, and the garrison continued in its peace-time role with a reasonably good expectation that Spain would not be hostile in a future war.

There were continuing friendly relations between the garrison and the local Spanish authorities. Smuggling did not cause much damage to local relations as there were many people on both sides of the border benefiting personally from it. Recreational activities were carried on in Spain and the Calpe Hunt flourished. The British sport of hunting took root in Spain in the eighteenth century, but the Calpe Hunt originated about 1812, when hounds were kept in San Roque under the mastership of the Reverend Mackareth. More hounds arrived in 1817 from the Duke of Wellington's pack, which had been stationed around Cadiz, and these were given to the 29th Regiment and the name Calpe Hunt adopted. Generally the garrison did not have much contact with civilians in Gibraltar, but the Calpe Hunt was an exception, as on the polo field. There was also some participation by leading Spanish families.

In Gibraltar itself social life became much more sophisticated and respectably Victorian than it had been in the days before the taverns were closed by the Duke of Kent. Garrison balls were a feature that at one time took place in the Club House (now the City Hall). The Club House itself had an interesting history in being originally a mansion built for Aaron Cardozo, a Jewish citizen; he was very helpful to the garrison in various ways, including getting supplies from Morocco at some danger to himself during the Napoleonic Wars. It was many years before he received the compensation promised, as he kept on having to start petitioning again whenever a governor, or lieutenant-governor, was replaced by a successor. Eventually the mansion rose, and after many changes it became the City Hall.

## THE NAVAL HARBOUR AND DOCKYARD

Towards the end of the nineteenth century the sea route to India and the Far East through the Suez Canal was carrying steadily increasing traffic. There was already a naval base at Malta, but there was a need for improved facilities at Gibraltar at the western end of the Mediterranean route; and work on the naval harbour and dockyard was begun in 1893. In 1901 Thomas Bowles, MP, suggested that work should be suspended on the 440-acre (178-hectare) harbour being constructed on the western side of the Rock on the grounds that the eastern side would be safer from bombardment from Spain; there was some controversy over the question but the harbour was completed in 10 years. Both King Edward VII and Queen Alexandra made separate visits and named drydocks. A tunnel 1,053yd (962·86m) long was driven through the Rock, and stone excavated from this and the reservoirs being constructed at the same time was used for the North and South Moles and the Detached Mole. The defences of the fortress were also modernised during the same period. Lower gun sites were abandoned in favour of higher sites with more range and a wider field of fire. In 1870 the guns of the Rock's defences were still smooth-bore weapons, with ranges limited to about 2 miles (3·22km), and the rifled bore guns developed after 1860 were only slowly brought into use.

## THE BOUNDARY FENCE

Spain was at war with the United States in 1898, largely around the Spanish possessions in the West Indies, but work was done on fortifications around Algeciras. The increasing range of guns was making British military experts more sensitive to the problems of hostile forces being on the Spanish mainland. Suggestions from Britain that the area should not be fortified did not produce any results, as Spain was still sensitive over Britain's possession of Gibraltar. Relations with Spain improved in 1906 when Alfonso XIII married Princess Victoria Eugénie of Battenburg, a granddaughter of Queen Victoria. In 1907 a declaration regarding the retention of present possessions was signed by Britain, France and Spain; there was also agreement to consult when international circumstances made it desirable.

The cordiality of relations received a setback in 1908, when the British Government informed the Spanish Government of its intention to erect a fence along the British edge of the neutral ground. There was no reaction from Spain for six months, and work had begun when the governor of Algeciras raised the question of the line of the fence. It was suggested that the line was north of that followed by British sentries for many years. Work continued when it had been confirmed that the fence did not go beyond the limits covered by sentries. In April 1909 the Spanish ambassador in London delivered a note stating that Spain only admitted British territory as being within the walls of the town ceded by the Treaty of Utrecht. A British reply in September 1909 (which remained unanswered) pointed out that there was no intention to depart from territorial arrangements observed on both sides over a long period. Developments on the isthmus had been taking place for over a century. Old maps and the model of the Rock in the Gibraltar Museum made in 1865 show that there was a substantial amount of development about half a century earlier. The fence did not serve much purpose at the time, except to reduce sentry duty, but erecting it showed a disregard for Spanish sensitivity when relations were good. The problem remained dormant for half a century, but it has come to the forefront in recent times.

Spain was neutral during World War I between 1914 and 1918. There was never any likelihood of Spain joining Germany against Britain and France, so that Gibraltar was a useful naval base far away from the great land battles in northern France. The harbour and the bay were used for inspecting shipping for contraband, for convoy collection and for patrols against submarines. The guns of the Rock rarely opened fire, as German submarines usually went through the Straits submerged, but there were fourteen 9·2in (23·37cm) guns, eleven 6in (15·24cm) guns and seven 4in (10·16cm) guns available for use. The maximum range of the 9·2in guns was about 15 miles (24·14km).

Navies of Britain's allies used the harbour during the war and in the latter stages the United States Navy was particularly in evidence. Cooperation with the United States is commemorated by the American War Memorial on Orange Bastion, and there is also a tablet to the USS *Chauncey*, which was sunk by a submarine in the Straits. Survivors from many ships were brought into Gibraltar during World War I. The greatest tragedy was perhaps the sinking of the battleship *Britannia* off the Spanish coast with 1,000 casualties two days before the Armistice of 11 November 1918.

The governor for nearly the whole of the period of the war was Lieutenant-General Sir Herbert Miles. He obtained whole-hearted support from Gibraltarians for the war effort and he maintained good relations with the governor of Algeciras. Spanish workers continued to come into Gibraltar, as they had done for 50 years, and there was no difficulty over obtaining food supplies from Spain.

RETURN TO PEACE

A few months before the end of World War I General Sir Horace Smith-Dorrien was appointed governor. He set a pattern followed by his successors in promoting progress for the civilian population, which had necessarily been neglected during the war years. The Civil Hospital was extended during Smith-Dorrien's period of office, but his work was perhaps more notable for the setting up of the City Council. When he took office, he was concerned by the problem of consulting the people whom he was governing. He put the matter to the Secretary of State and elections were held in December 1921 to fill four seats on a City Council, on which there were also five nominated members. A modest start had been made towards representation of the people in government. The functions of the Council included the duties formerly carried out by the Sanitary Commissioners, who had achieved some necessary improvements in the town during half a century, including the provision of a supply of drinkable water. The need for representation of the people was regarded by Smith-Dorrien as important for efficient administration, and in 1922 an executive council was set up. Unofficial members were appointed by the governor, although an official majority was maintained. In some ways Smith-Dorrien's period of office was marked by advances only comparable to those made in Don's time after the Napoleonic Wars. Without exception governors were senior army officers and they naturally put their garrison duties first, but some had vision beyond purely military needs.

The City Council was installed in the City Hall in 1924 by the next governor, General Sir Charles Monro. A request was made to him in 1926 for an unofficial majority on the Council, but he did not recommend it to the Secretary of State. General Sir Alexander Godley succeeded Sir Charles Monro in 1928, and some necessary public works, including a new market, were carried out in his time. The Gibraltar Museum was opened in 1930 and the Montagu Mixed Bathing Pavilion was set up in the same year; mixed bathing was previously only possible on the eastern side of the Rock, and a permit from the garrison adjutant was said to have been needed previously for a man to go bathing with his wife.

Commerce during the inter-war years was closely related

to the activities of the port. There was a steady decline in shipping using the port after World War I, the tonnage cleared between 1920 and 1923 falling from 11 million tons to 5 million tons per annum, but it slowly increased after that and reached 11 million tons again in 1934. Providing bunkering and other services was the main activity, but by 1934 a tourist industry based partly on cruising lines and partly on winter visitors from Britain was developing. Other activities were centred upon supplying goods and services to the garrison and smuggling into Spain.

The garrison usually consisted of two infantry battalions as well as Royal Artillery units. The main event of the year was the spring meeting of the Mediterranean and Home Fleets in Gibraltar. The strategic concept was one of a naval base on the long sea route to the Far East. Large battleships and many cruisers and destroyers gave at least the impression that the sea route would remain safe for commerce.

### WAR CLOUDS GATHER AGAIN

In October 1935 the dispute between Italy and Abyssinia developed into open war. Some naval precautions were taken in the Mediterranean, and reinforcements from the Home Fleet passed through Gibraltar on the way to the eastern Mediterranean. Italian troops were, however, allowed to use the Suez Canal freely, and an opportunity to stop a dictator was lost. The Abyssinian war demonstrated that air power was becoming of increasing significance, and this led to a realisation that Gibraltar's air defences needed improving.

War came much nearer in July 1936, when the Spanish Civil War began. General Franco led the uprising in Morocco and other Spanish generals led similar risings in Seville, Algeciras and elsewhere. In the area around Gibraltar the main objective of the Nationalist forces led by General Franco was to transport Moroccan troops to Spain. Some warships of the Spanish navy, including the *Jaime I*, were taken over by their crews in support of the Republican Government, which led to some confusion when they sought fuel supplies at

Gibraltar. The ships' officers had either been killed or imprisoned below decks, but the crews claimed to be supporting a government trying to suppress a revolution. Supplies were refused. There was an air attack on the ships and some pieces of shrapnel from anti-aircraft fire landed on the Rock. A British protest was most courteously answered by a visit to apologise from one of the local Spanish commanders.

There was some fighting in La Linea just across the border, and a front developed to the north of San Roque. Thousands of refugees came into Gibraltar and a camp was established on the racecourse situated on the isthmus. The refugee problem was a serious one for an already overcrowded place, but it lessened substantially when the Nationalist forces took Malaga in February 1937. Throughout the civil war there were always about 2,000 refugees in Gibraltar, but in its very early days there were about 10,000.

After the capture of Malaga the garrison was again able to resume visits to Spain, and signs of war on land lessened. At sea an international patrol was established off the Spanish coasts to prevent intervention by outside powers. This patrol was composed of ships from the navies of Britain, France, Germany and Italy. Some ships suffered damage while on patrol duties, including the British destroyer *Hunter*, which was towed into Gibraltar in May 1937 in a sinking condition after striking a mine. Another ship that came into Gibraltar after being damaged was the German battleship *Deutschland*, whose dead were buried at Gibraltar but later exhumed to be buried in Germany on Hitler's orders. In August 1937 Admiral Rolf Carls came, on the battleship *Admiral Scheer*, to convey thanks to the governor, General Sir Charles Harrington, for the help given to the *Deutschland* and her wounded sailors.

While courtesies were exchanged with German ships using Gibraltar during the Spanish Civil War, the employment of German and Italian air power in Spain did not pass unnoticed. These forces were present in defiance of the principles of non-intervention, and their effectiveness demonstrated the nakedness of the Rock in air defence: at the time it had no landing ground for fighter aircraft, and the civil population in the crowded area of the town would have been very vulnerable to air attack.

Sir Charles Harrington had to deal with some formidable problems during his governorship. The Spanish Civil War brought refugees with differing views on the war into Gibraltar, but the high degree of impartiality maintained enabled relations with the local Spanish authorities to remain on the usual friendly footing. The Calpe Hunt was once again a source of good relations. Lady Harrington had the distinction of being the first lady master, when she held the post jointly with the Marques de Marzales, who lived in Algeciras.

In August 1938 there was a naval action off the eastern side of the Rock between the Spanish Government destroyer *Jose Luis Diez* and the Nationalist cruiser *Canarias*. The destroyer was trying to enter the Mediterranean, but she was badly damaged by the cruiser, and turned back, managing to get into Gibraltar harbour by keeping very close to Europa Point. Some effort had been made to disguise the destroyer as a British ship, but this failed to deceive the captain of the *Canarias*. The *Jose Luis Diez* was interned for the rest of the war.

The Spanish Civil War brought up the question of Gibraltar's usefulness as a naval base. The possibility of making an exchange for Ceuta had been raised after World War I, when dependence on Spanish neutrality was apparent. The issue was still alive during the Civil War, when the placing of four howitzers near Algeciras caused excitement in the British press; but a much more serious problem at the time of the Munich crisis of September 1938 was the presence of German and Italian air force units in Spain. This made the building of an air strip on land occupied by the racecourse on the isthmus an urgent matter; strengthening anti-aircraft defences and civil defence measures also required attention. These tasks were energetically set in hand by General Sir Edmund Ironside when he became governor in 1938.

## WORLD WAR II

World War II began quietly for Gibraltar. The Spanish Civil War had ended in April 1939, and the German and Italian air force units had left Spain when World War II started in September. Italy initially kept out of the war, so that the Rock was far removed from all fighting fronts, and quickly assumed its World War I role as a place for examining ships for contraband and a centre for convoy collection.

The situation changed rapidly after the German invasion of France and the Low Countries in May 1940. French resistance collapsed in June and by that time Italy had declared war. German forces reached the Pyrenees, and French North Africa came under the Vichy Government. Plans prepared for evacuating the civil population from Gibraltar, except for about 4,000 persons required for defence works and essential services, were put into effect, and over 14,000 went. Some were sent to Casablanca but they later had to go to England, where those who went to London found the air raids worse than anything that happened in Gibraltar. Later in the war some Gibraltarians went to camps in Northern Ireland. The accommodation was uncomfortable, but many Gibraltarians have memories of being warmly welcomed there. From a point of view of a climate more like their own, Gibraltarians evacuated to Jamaica were the most fortunate; they were also far removed from air raids, and they happened to be among the first to return home.

There were a few Italian air raids on Gibraltar, which caused some casualties and damage to buildings, but there was little interference with the operational activities of the port and naval harbour. Royal Navy units used the base to retain control of the western Mediterranean and provide relief for Malta, which was close to a hostile Italy. The action against the French fleet at Oran was mounted from Gibraltar. At the time it seemed necessary, but it was the source of much bitterness between former allies, and a strong factor in persuading some 3,000 French troops who had been evacuated to Gibraltar not to continue in the war with Britain.

In October 1940 Hitler met General Franco at Hendaye, and asked for permission for German troops to pass through Spain and take control of the Straits of Gibraltar. After the failure to invade Britain in 1940, cutting her communications with the western Mediterranean and denying her the use of Gibraltar would have been one of the most severe blows that Germany could deliver. General Franco refused permission, although he had been making pro-German speeches and had described his country as non-belligerent as opposed to neutral. From a Spanish point of view there were dangers in letting German troops enter Spain, for there were still guerrilla groups, particularly among the Basques and Catalans, who might have become active again. Spain needed to recover from the Civil War, and there might have been difficulty in persuading the Germans to leave Spain if Hitler won the war. General Franco was not convinced that Hitler would win the war, so he thought it best to keep out of it. The chance of recovering Gibraltar had some attractions, but Britain's counter-action would have been to seize the Canary Islands, and neither Germany nor Spain would have had the necessary naval forces to prevent this.

It would have been possible for Germany to go through Spain without Spanish consent, but there would have been risks on the long lines of communication. These dangers could probably have been met by Germany in 1940, but after the invasion of Russia in June 1941 greatly reduced German forces were available. Thus the threat to the Rock receded. In the view of some strategists Hitler's failure to take control of the Iberian Peninsula and North Africa was one of his big mistakes.

When the danger to Gibraltar had receded, work was put in hand to prepare it as an offensive base for operations in North Africa. Much tunnelling was done within the Rock and material dug out was used to extend the runway of the airfield out into the sea on the western side of the isthmus. After the United States came into the war in December 1941, preparations for the invasion of North Africa proceeded as the allied Operation Torch. By the time General Eisenhower arrived in Gibraltar in November 1942 a tremendous concentration of sea and air power had been effected. There was the danger of a pre-emptive attack on Gibraltar by Germany, but none took place, and Operation Torch went ahead as the first successful Anglo-American combined operation. It was also the first time that British forces fought under General Eisenhower.

The war at sea around Gibraltar was waged constantly from 1939 until the German surrender in May 1945. Before the operations against North Africa were undertaken, a major task had been escorting convoys to Malta. In August 1942 Operation Pedestal proved particularly costly in naval and merchant vessels, for the convoy was reported to the Germans when it passed through the Straits of Gibraltar and as a result was under constant attack thereon by submarines and aircraft. Only five supply ships reached Malta, including the tanker *Ohio*, which was of vital importance in the relief of the beleaguered island. Nine supply ships were sunk, as well as an aircraft carrier, two cruisers and a destroyer.

There were heavy losses throughout the war around Gibraltar from submarine action. Midget submarines attacked shipping in the convoy-collecting area of the bay and added to the toll taken in the Straits and off the Spanish and African coasts. The loss of the aircraft carrier *Ark Royal* within 25 miles (40·23km) of the Rock in November 1941 was a heavy blow at a time when Britain was suffering severely at sea. The Royal Navy tried hard, as in World War I, to prevent the passage of submarines through the Straits, but it was not an easy task.

During the last few years of the war Gibraltar became an important staging post in allied air communications. It was used as such by King George VI when visiting troops in North Africa. The air strip was not ideal for large-scale operations, and the hazards of air currents around the Rock were present, although they apply less seriously to operations from the isthmus than to those of seaplanes from the harbour. It is not surprising that there were some accidents, one of which, in July 1943, resulted in the death of the Polish commander General Sikorski.

The runway at the present-day airport is perhaps the most impressive monument of work done in World War II. There are still some old wartime pillboxes, resembling some built in Britain in 1940, but they are much less impressive than the Moorish Castle or the great bastions of the eighteenth and nineteenth century. There is, however, much underground work, which cannot be visited by the public.

The war ended quietly in Gibraltar, with atom bombs dropped on far away Hiroshima and Nagasaki. The advent of such obliterative weapons, however, posed a big problem for a base such as Gibraltar. The range from which it could be rendered untenable had suddenly increased to the range of an aircraft carrying one bomb.

# 6       THE DISPUTED ROCK

AT the end of World War II the Rock seemed more British than ever before. Spain had been non-belligerent, but the country was governed by a military dictator who had expressed support for Hitler's Germany; and the idea that Spain might even consider claiming sovereignty over Gibraltar was far removed from anybody's thoughts in Britain. In the area of Spain around Gibraltar relations were on a friendly basis, so that in 1945 a dispute with Spain appeared very unlikely.

There was a dispute from 1944 onwards between the British Government and representatives of the Gibraltarians over the repatriation of the civilians evacuated in 1940. During the earlier years of the war the civilians who had remained on the Rock accepted the same dangers as the garrison. They were subjected to a number of petty irritations, such as exclusion from garrison entertainments, but the greatest hardship was separation from their families after Gibraltar had become far removed from any battlefront. In April 1944 some of the wives and children of men who had remained in Gibraltar were repatriated, an event followed by a demonstration calling for quicker repatriation. One result was the removal of the Gibraltarians from London to Northern Ireland, where they were out of range of flying bombs and rockets, but the return of all Gibraltarians was a very slow process. A shortage of shipping was the main difficulty, but there was perhaps a disregard of civilian needs, and demonstrations continued until the end of 1947, when some Gibraltarians had still not returned home. The process was not completed until 1951.

## POLITICAL ADVANCES

Before the end of World War II there was an acceptance in Britain of a need for political advancement in countries under colonial rule. In 1944 the proposals for Gibraltar were based upon parity in numbers on the City Council of elected members with official and nominated members, but this did not go far enough for the Association for the Advancement of Civil Rights, which had been formed under the leadership of Mr J. A. Hassan (now Sir Joshua Hassan). His family had been established in Gibraltar for many generations, so that he was well placed to fight for the acceptance of the principle of an elected majority. He achieved this concession from the British Government and his party won all the seven seats allocated to elected members on the City Council in 1945. Representation only on a City Council did not, however, satisfy Gibraltarians at a time when India, Pakistan and Ceylon were becoming self-governing, and eventually agreement was reached with the British Government on the setting up of a Legislative Council. This was constituted by an Order in Council of 3 February 1950, and composed of the governor as president, a speaker, three ex-officio members, two nominated members and seven elected members. The governor remained the executive authority, but an executive council was set up under his chairmanship with four official members and four elected members.

Gibraltar had a reminder of its military nature in 1951, when a lighter containing ammunition exploded in the harbour. The lighter lay alongside the naval supply ship *Bedenham*. Fortunately the ship itself sank and did not explode, but the damage caused by the disaster was greater than that resulting from air raids during World War II. Many houses were damaged, the east window of the Cathedral of the Holy Trinity was shattered and much destruction occurred in the Army Ordnance Depot, which stood on the site now occupied by the John Mackintosh Hall. Thirteen people were killed and many more were injured. The incident brought back war-time memories, but political matters were now in the forefront.

Constitutional changes in Gibraltar were watched with some apprehension in Spain. There were moves towards self-government in many British colonies and it was thought in Spain that this would prejudice the chances of recovering Gibraltar. A short visit to Gibraltar by Queen Elizabeth II in 1954 led to a Spanish protest and the withdrawal of the Spanish consul. Restrictions were imposed on Spanish workers going into Gibraltar from La Linea under which no new passes were to be allowed. The employment of Spanish workers in Gibraltar had been going on for nearly a century, and had continued with very little hindrance during the Spanish Civil War and World War II. During World War II the number employed increased from about 8,000 to a peak figure of 13,000, and over 12,000 persons were crossing the border daily when the restrictions were imposed. As wages were better in Gibraltar and there was a shortage of work in La Linea, the decline in numbers was only gradual.

### UNO CALLS FOR DECOLONISATION

There were diplomatic exchanges between Britain and Spain concerning Gibraltar over the years following 1954, but nothing was achieved. In September 1963 the question came before the United Nations Special Committee on Decolonisation, before which Sir Joshua Hassan and Mr Peter Isola as Gibraltarian representatives were allowed to appear. They stated that they did not wish for any changes in sovereignty and that they had already achieved a large degree of self-government. The debate was adjourned and in August 1964 a revised constitution abolished the executive council and replaced it with a Gibraltar Council on which there was an unofficial majority.

The Special Committee debate was resumed in September 1964, and despite further Gibraltarian representations, a resolution was passed calling on Britain and Spain to negotiate. On 17 October, a day after the resolution was passed, the

Spanish authorities at La Linea began to make crossing the frontier a more difficult and slower process. The British Government regarded these restrictions as amounting to duress and no negotiations took place. In December 1965 the General Assembly of UNO passed a resolution calling upon Britain and Spain to hold talks, and about the same time the Spanish *Red Book* on Gibraltar was published. This has been followed by another *Red Book* in 1968 and by British white papers published between 1965 and 1968.

Talks between Britain and Spain began in May 1966. The Spanish asked for the rescission of the Treaty of Utrecht and the return of Gibraltar. They also submitted proposals for the Gibraltarians to continue under their own civil laws, religions and other institutions operating under a town council which would raise its own taxes; Gibraltarians would be granted reciprocal rights of residence with Spaniards; and Britain would be allowed to continue to use the naval base and military installations. But in January 1966 NATO countries had been informed that their military aircraft could not fly over Spain on the way to Gibraltar, in August female workers were prevented from entering Gibraltar, and in October the frontier gates were closed to vehicles.

In December the matter came before the Fourth Committee of the General Assembly of UNO, to which the Committee on Decolonisation had submitted a report. A resolution was passed calling on Britain to expedite, in consultation with Spain, the decolonisation of Gibraltar. The resolution made a reference to the need to take the interests of the people into account and Britain voted for the resolution on this basis.

In September 1967 a referendum was held. The people of Gibraltar were asked to say which of the following alternative courses would best serve their interests:

A.  To pass under Spanish sovereignty in accordance with the terms proposed by the Spanish Government to Her Majesty's Government on 18th May 1966, or
B.  Voluntarily to retain their link with Britain with demo-

cratic local institutions and with Britain retaining its present responsibilities.

The referendum was administered by Sir Robert Fowler. A Commonwealth team of observers unanimously reported that the referendum gave free expression of choice through a secret ballot. The result was 44 votes for A and 12,138 votes for B, leaving Britain in no doubt about how the people of Gibraltar viewed their interests.

Proposed talks between Britain and Spain were postponed twice during 1967, and none took place. The first postponement came when Spain announced a prohibited air zone to come into operation in May; later Spain asked to postpone the talks until after the matter had come before the United Nations in December. The Fourth Committee condemned the referendum as being contrary to previous resolutions, and invited Britain to decolonise Gibraltar in accordance with paragraph 6 of Resolution 1514 (XV). The paragraph reads:

6. Any attempt aimed at the partial or total disruption of the national unity and the territorial integrity of a country is incompatible with the purposes and principles of the Charter of the United Nations.

No reference was made to paragraph 2, which reads:

2. All peoples have the right to self-determination; by virtue of that right they freely determine their political status and freely pursue their economic, social and cultural development.

There is a conflict between the two paragraphs when they are applied to Gibraltar. Territorially Gibraltar was part of Spain until the Treaty of Utrecht in 1713. The Spanish case is based on territory, but the people of Gibraltar do not want to become politically united with Spain under any proposals put forward so far. Britain's case is based upon people who have freely expressed their wishes in a referendum.

Several years elapsed before there were further talks with Spain, but Sir Alec Douglas-Home took up the subject again with the Spanish Foreign Minister, Don Gregorio Lopez Bravo, in 1971. There were further inconclusive talks, but these were suspended after about a year. In the meantime, in June 1969, Spain had prevented the remaining Spanish labour force of 4,666 men from crossing the frontier into Gibraltar and the last link, the Algeciras–Gibraltar ferry service, was withdrawn later in the month. Telephone and telegraph services were cut on 1 October 1969.

THE SPANISH CASE

The Spanish case for the return of Gibraltar and proposals for Gibraltarians have undergone some changes over the years since 1950, when Gibraltar was granted a Legislative Council. The original Spanish case was based partly on the provisions of the Treaty of Utrecht giving preference to Spain in the event of Britain relinquishing Gibraltar. There was also the question of encroachment on to the isthmus, and Britain has been willing to refer problems arising from the treaty to the International Court of Justice at The Hague. Spain declined to do this after the United Nations had called for the decolonisation of Gibraltar. The Spanish case is now based on the UNO call for decolonisation, which in its present form appears to mean handing Gibraltar back to Spain whatever the interests or wishes of the people may be.

Some revised suggestions for Gibraltarians were given to Sir Joshua Hassan in 1973, but there was no great change from the previous position. Gibraltarians would have a town council to replace their present government and they would have to accept Spanish sovereignty. Economically they would benefit from the opening of the frontier, but the large majority of Gibraltarians still wish to remain under the British Crown. As long as they remain subjects of the Crown, and Gibraltar is within the Queen's dominions, there is little substance in the Spanish contention that Britain was giving up Gibraltar by granting local self-government to Gibraltarians. Self-government over a wide range of matters does not affect the status of Gibraltar under the Crown.

If Spain had agreed to put the dispute over the Treaty of Utrecht to the International Court, there would have been a judicial decision covering subjects that have caused much confusion. Instead there is only a politically motivated resolution by the United Nations Organisation calling for decolonisation by handing over Gibraltar to Spain. If this were to be done, it would infringe the principle of self-determination for the people of colonial territories. On the Spanish side it is argued that the Gibraltarians are not a people who should have self-determination. They are regarded by Spain as a population that has settled in a fortress. How far they have a right to self-determination needs to be considered in the light of their history, their culture, their laws and their institutions.

Are the Gibraltarians a people? Britain's case against handing over Gibraltar to Spain rests on an affirmative answer to this question.

# 7    THE GIBRALTARIANS

THE EXPERIENCE of being evacuated from Gibraltar during World War II was not a pleasant one for the 14,000 people who had to leave their homes, but it had the advantage of bringing the existence of Gibraltarians to the notice of people in Britain. Previously they had usually been known only to British people who had lived in Gibraltar, and even for them there was some confusion about the ancestry of Gibraltarians. A few years after World War II Dr H. W. Howes, a Director of Education in Gibraltar, carried out research on registers of inhabitants and census reports, and the results are now available in his book *The Gibraltarian*.

Dr Howes, took the year 1704 as his starting point. Although a few Genoese and a smaller number of Spaniards remained after the British and Dutch forces captured Gibraltar, the year 1704 marked the beginning of a new population.

### THE EIGHTEENTH CENTURY

The eighteenth-century sieges and other wars that might have led to hostilities around Gibraltar discouraged much growth of population. The general pattern of development of a Gibraltarian population was, however, established during the eighteenth century before the Napoleonic Wars.

There was not much immigration during the period 1704–27. In 1721 there were 310 citizens able to bear arms – 45 Englishmen, 96 Spaniards and 169 Genoese. After the siege of 1727 the rate of immigration increased, but little information is available about the first half of the century. In 1753 there was a total civilian population of 1,816 persons, of whom 83 were British civilians connected with the navy, 351 were other British civilians, 597 were Genoese, 575 were Jews, 185 were Spaniards and 25 were Portuguese. The Jews were mostly from Morocco, with which trading had become established – fresh food supplies were imported and manufactured goods originating from Britain exported. Gibraltar had been declared a free port during Queen Anne's reign, partly to encourage the Moroccan trade, which had attracted the Jews, as trading people, and the seafaring Genoese and Portuguese.

The development of commerce useful to Britain was favoured by such governors as General Bland, who held office from 1749 to 1751. He wrote in his notes for his successor that Protestants should be encouraged to settle and take part in commercial development, as he regarded them as a source of strength for the garrison. Roman Catholics, however, continued to predominate, as they still do now. A register of 1767 shows that there were 467 British civilians, who were probably nearly all Protestants, 1,460 Roman Catholics of non-British nationality and 783 Jews, making up a total population of 2,710. The details of the register at this time concentrated on religious categories, but there is more detail in the register of 1777, when the total population was 3,201. A division was then made between native British Protestants, native Roman Catholics and native Jews, as opposed to non-natives in the same categories. There were 1,332 persons classified as natives and 1,869 as non-natives. Among 519 British, 220 were classified as natives, constituting a British population developed from members of the garrison settling after service in Gibraltar. They became known as 'Rock scorpions'.

The Great Siege of 1779–83 had an effect on the composition of the population as some citizens left with the relieving ships that brought reinforcements and supplies. A register of 1787 shows a small increase in population over the figure for 1777, but out of a total of 3,386 there was a decline in the number of Jews from 863 to 776; this can be attributed to the loss of trading opportunities during the siege. Lists of names compiled during the siege distinguished between Latin and Hebrew ones. Many of these names are still well known ones in Gibraltar, although this does not of course show ancestry going back to this time. Bassadone and Baglietto are examples of Genoese names in the register, Garcia is one of the Spanish names, and Hassan, Levy and Serfaty are Hebrew.

## THE NAPOLEONIC WARS AND THEIR AFTERMATH

Another register of population was compiled in 1791. This was the end of the period of the small-scale growth of the eighteenth century and the beginning of the developments of the Napoleonic Wars. In 1791 there had been a fall of population to 2,890 from the figure of 3,386 for 1787, owing to the French Revolution's effect on trade since 1789. A change soon occurred as a result of the exclusion of British ships from some Mediterranean ports during the Napoleonic Wars, but the register of 1791 gave useful details of both the occupations and the original homes of the population. There was a widening range of nationalities represented in the population and Italians (other than Genoese), Minorcans, Maltese, French and Sicilians were becoming more prominent. A tendency for some of the larger groups of people to settle in their own national areas was also evident. The British, for example, were situated around King's Bastion, whereas the Spanish and Portuguese occupied the Cooperage District near the Waterport.

During the Napoleonic Wars Gibraltar's trade developed from small-scale importing and exporting to large-scale entre-pôt activities. By 1801 the population had risen to 5,339, having nearly doubled in 10 years; and in the next 10 years up to 1811 it more than doubled to reach 11,173. By 1813 the population had risen to 12,423, but persons who had not obtained permission to reside in Gibraltar were expelled later in the year, and in 1814 the total fell to 10,136. A yellow fever epidemic in 1813 also played a part, as it had in 1804, and by November 1814 14,900 people had suffered from the disease, and nearly half had died.

When the population was growing rapidly during the Napoleonic Wars, the religions of the population began to assume a secondary place in the registers to their occupations and national origins. In the trades sections of the registers a gradual move can be observed towards the classification of more people as natives, as opposed to their original nationalities. Another interesting development is the increase in the number of Minorcans in trades between 1814 and 1834. During much of the eighteenth century Minorca had been British, but by the time it was finally returned to Spain in 1802 it had acquired a cosmopolitan population of its own.

The register of trades is also interesting from the point of view of the occupations followed by different sections of the community. In 1834 natives were in the lead among carpenters, coopers, cigar-makers and seamstresses, while Genoese were the most numerous among bakers and gardeners. The Spanish element was very widely spread, showing less concentration in particular occupations. A trade of remarkable size for a small place was cigar-making, which was carried on as a cottage type of industry and occupied no less than 540 persons. Sales across the border in Spain with the aid of smugglers were the main source of income for this trade. Smugglers were a floating community, but in 1834 one person dared to register as a resident smuggler. Major Hort, writing in 1839, describes smugglers as being evident in the streets 'arrayed in their fanciful yet picturesque costumes'.

### NINETEENTH-CENTURY DEVELOPMENTS

The total population reached a peak about 1831, when a register of inhabitants showed there were 17,024. A census in 1834 gave a total figure of 15,002, the substantial reduction in three years being partly caused by declining trade and partly by a cholera epidemic during 1834. There were 380 deaths, and quarantine restrictions cut down movements of people into Gibraltar.

By 1844 the population had risen slightly to 15,823. A new classification was adopted in that year, into British and alien populations. There were 12,182 British and 3,641 aliens. The former category was broken down into 995 persons of British Isles stock, including service families, 9,802 natives and 1,385 British and native Jews. Amongst the aliens there were 1,892 Spaniards, 782 Genoese, 525 Portuguese and 240 Barbary Jews. The remaining 202 came from many different countries, including France and Italy.

The process of aliens gradually becoming assimilated as natives continued throughout the nineteenth century, but the main elements of the native population had become established by 1844. Cholera epidemics affected the total numbers from time to time, but there was in general a steady rise in numbers. The census of 1871 showed that the total population had reached 18,695.

Overcrowding within the fortress had been causing anxiety to governors for some years, but little had been done to prevent it, although Sir Robert Gardiner had suggested drastic action to curb smuggling into Spain, which was the source of livelihood for many civilians. In 1873 an Aliens Order in Council was made under which only British persons could enter freely. 'British' included persons from other parts of the Empire than Britain, and the Order resulted in a substantial immigration from Malta. There was much resentment against this, as there were stronger links with Spain than there were with Malta, from where relatively few inhabitants of Gibraltar had come up until 1873. The Maltese were stated by some, including the Roman Catholic Vicar Apostolic, Dr J. B. Scandella, to be responsible for much of the crime of the city. This was not, however, borne out by the statistics, although Maltese goatherds, like pastoral people elsewhere, were before the courts from time to time for allowing their animals to wander on to other people's property. There is now a Maltese element in the Gibraltarian population and names such as Cassar, Mifsud and Zammitt are usually representative of Maltese ancestry. The study of names, however, does not give conclusive results, as there were many migrations in the Mediterranean during the time that the Gibraltarian population was coming together.

The opening of the Suez Canal in 1869 did not result in rapid commercial developments in Gibraltar, and the period between 1870 and 1890 was not a particularly prosperous one, but after 1890 dockyard developments leading to the construction of the naval harbour brought about a substantial change. There was a need for more labour, some of which came in from Spain, but many Gibraltarians found skilled and unskilled employment. Between 1891 and 1901 the civilian population increased from 19,000 to 20,355, and there were by this time several thousand workers coming in daily from Spain. There were 14,761 persons classified as natives of Gibraltar, while among the remainder 1,309 persons were from Britain, 1,628 from other British countries and 2,657 classified as aliens.

## THE TWENTIETH CENTURY

Between 1901 and 1961 there was a census every 10 years, except in 1941. The figures, which exclude service families, do not show any great variations, but there was a gradual decline from 20,355 in 1901 to 17,405 in 1931. In 1951 the population was 20,845, and it reached 21,636 in 1961. The next census was in 1970, soon after the Spanish frontier closure had made it necessary for Gibraltar to accommodate all its work force. The population was 24,672 and the increase made further housing development necessary. Since World War II housing estates have been built outside the walls of the town, a departure from former times, when it was customary for nearly all civilians, apart from some service families, to live within the town area.

## CATALAN BAY

The village of Catalan Bay on the eastern side of the Rock is still the most marked exception to the concentration of population in the town area or just outside it in the new housing estates. The village probably began as a summer-season settlement for Genoese fishermen, for the bay provided a good beach for boats and a place with comparatively little danger from landslides from the sandy slopes above it. Although Catalan Bay was originally a Genoese settlement, the register of 1814 shows that the population had become much more mixed, and Spaniards and Portuguese were also there at that time. About 250 people now live in Catalan Bay. There has been little change in the total population or in the separateness of the community in recent years. Catalan Bay residents rarely go to live around the other side, as it is known, there is a tendency for marriages to take place within the community, and village customs have also been preserved. On the other hand, it has for a long time been the practice for men to go to work in the dockyard and elsewhere in Gibraltar.

The most marked change in Catalan Bay in recent years has been its adaptation to the tourist industry. There is much less fishing done now than there was, and a bonito net hung from the ceiling of a small tavern on the sea front is perhaps symbolic of this change. The Caleta Palace Hotel, which stands on a rocky piece of coast just south of the village, largely accounts for the new role of catering for tourists, who can obtain drinks, light refreshments and meals in the village. They can bathe from the sandy beach or take boat trips out to sea with the local fishermen.

## GIBRALTARIAN CULTURE

The ancestry of Gibraltarians from British, Genoese, Spanish, Portuguese, Minorcan, Italian and Maltese stock, among others, has naturally resulted in their culture being drawn from many sources. In recent years British and Spanish influences have predominated. The Spanish style can be seen in some buildings and in dress, particularly among the older women. The Spanish language has a long history from the time the Moors were expelled, and it is still used in many homes. English has now become the medium of instruction in schools, and the closure of the frontier will in time affect the use of Spanish; but during the long period that the frontier was open Spanish was the language for commerce in Gibraltar. The Roman Catholic religion has also continued strongly, as it has in Spain and in some other Mediterranean lands. In the 1970 Census Report 19,133 persons are classified as Roman Catholics, which represents over three-quarters of the civil population, apart from families of the garrison. Persons belonging to other Christian churches numbered 2,418, there were 1,989 Moslems (mostly Moroccans) and 552 persons of the Jewish faith.

In music the Spanish influence is strong, but in drama and the cinema there is a more British taste and interest, which has been developed by the greater use of English in recent years. Another move in developing a taste in British arts resulted from the setting up of the John Mackintosh Hall in 1964. John Mackintosh was born in 1865 and left money in trust when he died in 1940 for the purpose of encouraging interest in British culture in Gibraltar. He was the son of a Scot who married a Gibraltarian, and was a successful businessman engaged in shipping enterprises both in the City of London and Gibraltar. He set up his own company in Gibraltar and was interested in many charitable works during his lifetime. The activities in John Mackintosh Hall are mostly cultural ones, but there is also a gymnasium. The hall provides a meeting place for many clubs and societies interested in such pursuits as drama, photography, stamp-collecting and chess. There is a library, and there are rooms for exhibiting paintings and for other artistic activities. The hall caters for recreations and interests that would often be found in an English town of similar size.

### GIBRALTARIAN INSTITUTIONS

The reasons for the Gibraltarian's preference for retaining his links with Britain rather than joining Spain are easier to find in his government, his institutions and his laws than in his culture. The instability of Spanish governments after World War I and the overthrow of the monarchy in 1931, when Alfonso XIII left the country, resulted in Gibraltarians tending to favour British institutions. The Popular Front government set up in Spain in 1931, and its actions against the Roman Catholic church, were viewed with distaste in Gibraltar; and the military regime that followed in southern Spain soon after the Civil War began in 1936 did not bring about any sudden improvement in feelings over Spanish politics.

As well as developing a government along British lines, Gibraltar trade unions have close British associations. There is a Trades Council on the TUC pattern and the Transport and General Workers Union has close links with the British union of that name.

The *Gibraltar Chronicle* is the oldest newspaper, and is British in style. It began in 1801 as a garrison newspaper, but is now independent. In 1968 it caused a popular demonstration by publishing a letter from certain citizens, who called themselves 'The Doves', proposing some form of bargain with Spain.

Education in Gibraltar also follows British lines, although it has a relatively short history. The first school was established by Sir George Don in 1820, for the children of members of the garrison. In 1831 the pattern of mission schools common in British colonies was begun by S. H. Rule, a Methodist. Big steps forward were made in the time of Dr Scandella, who became Roman Catholic Vicar Apostolic in 1855. He set up a school for boys and another for girls in which English was taught as well as Spanish and other languages. From Dr Scandella's time onwards there was a steady development of education on the lines being followed in Britain.

Educational policy is now the responsibility of the Minister of Education. At the top of the educational ladder come a boys' comprehensive school and a separate girls' comprehensive school. Below these there are eleven primary and middle schools catering respectively for children of five to eight and eight to twelve years. There is a technical college, two private schools and two schools for the children of members of the services. There is also a school for mentally handicapped children, a government nursery school and about a dozen private nursery schools.

Children are required to attend school between the ages of five and fifteen years, and those with the necessary ability can continue for as long as they can benefit. University education takes place in Britain or elsewhere outside Gibraltar. There are scholarships and grants for such studies, and it is the policy to provide education in Gibraltar for those who can qualify for entry to institutions overseas.

Careful attention is given to the health of schoolchildren, and a special service for children forms part of the government health services. These services include St Bernard's Hospital, with over 180 beds, and the King George V Psychiatric Unit, with accommodation for over 60 patients. There are arrangements by which hospitals in Britain take patients if the treatment required cannot be given in Gibraltar, and visits to Gibraltar are sometimes made by British specialists. A comprehensive medical service on the basis of that in Britain has not yet been established, but it is the aim.

### THE GIBRALTARIAN WAY OF LIFE

The Gibraltarian way of life is predominantly British and middle class in style. A number of Gibraltarians have acquired wealth, but they usually live unostentatiously. At the other end of the scale there are few Gibraltarians in unskilled labouring jobs; Spaniards formerly did most of these jobs and now their place has been taken by Moroccans. Gibraltarians have continued to work mainly in government, business and shops, and in skilled jobs in which they are very industrious.

The new housing estates built since World War II have brought about great improvements in living standards, but some adaptation to life in high blocks of flats has been necessary. The old style of large houses in which people rented one or two rooms had a social life of its own, for people lived much closer to each other than they do in self-contained flats.

A few of the older style of houses exist in the area between Casemates Square and Moorish Castle, which contains the worst housing in Gibraltar by modern standards, though the people manifest their loyalty to Britain strongly. Many inscriptions on walls have demonstrated this, the most succinct being 'OK with UK'. There was a strong dislike of the style of government exercised by General Franco of Spain, and the new regime is being watched with interest. The bars in the area, such as that of the Artillery Arms, provide meeting places for discussions on politics and many subjects after working hours. These bars are staffed and frequented almost entirely by Gibraltarian men, but the taverns in Main Street are often staffed by barmen and barmaids from Britain, and largely used by ships' crews, members of the garrison, tourists and others from outside Gibraltar.

The family influence is very strong in Gibraltar, and this extends to brothers, sisters, cousins and aunts as well as to the immediate circle of husband, wife and children. Sunday is a family day, and the Roman Catholic churches are well attended for mass. Before the frontier was closed, family picnics in Spain were common, but now the Gibraltar beaches and the Upper Rock have to take the place of Spanish territory. The Upper Rock has a remoteness from the crowded town and a contrasting peacefulness arising from its woodland nature and distant views across the sea.

On Sunday evening Main Street is full of husbands and wives, and lasses and lads, out walking. The young men no longer dress in the conventional Sunday best, but the girls continue to make themselves look attractive. As daughters tend to be watched for the company they keep, there is a courting problem for young people, and in a small place there is little chance of young people going out together without their parents knowing. Scooters and small cars are much prized by young men wishing to escort their girl friends around the Rock.

For young people the world outside Gibraltar seems to give more scope. Overseas scholarships awarded by the government usually require an undertaking to return to work for a period. Some young people leave after this time, so there is sometimes a loss of talent, but a few return again later after experience elsewhere.

There is not much room on the Rock for sport, but football, hockey and basketball are all played and enthusiastically supported. Around the coasts there is plenty of scope for sea sports such as swimming, rowing and sailing. The government takes a keen interest in sport and there is a minister concerned with it. One holder of the office, Mr Zammitt, has the personal distinction of having swum across the Straits of Gibraltar.

Some Gibraltarians go on holiday visits to the United Kingdom, where many have relatives and friends, and others visit relatives in Spain and elsewhere. A day trip across the Straits to Tangier and back in the *Mons Calpe* also provides a break from the confinement of Gibraltar. This is something felt by Gibraltarians, but generally accepted cheerfully. When families are divided by the frontier, the separation seems cruel, but paying the price of joining Spain to get over this is seldom contemplated.

### GIBRALTARIAN STATUS

The law on Gibraltarian status could have been very complicated, considering the mixed ancestry of Gibraltarians, but the Gibraltarian Status Ordnance gets over the difficulties neatly by defining a Gibraltarian as a person registered as a Gibraltarian. Anyone born in Gibraltar before 30 June 1925 has a right to be registered, as may descendants of males born in Gibraltar before that date and wives and widows of such descendants. The Governor in Council has powers to register persons of British descent who speak English and are of good character as Gibraltarians, but this power is sparingly used. Gibraltarian status is associated with a distinctive background of ancestry, history and institutions, but the laws and government now require more detailed examination.

# 8 LAW, GOVERNMENT AND FINANCE

FOR 16 years after the British capture Gibraltar lacked any properly constituted civil courts, but the Prince of Hesse appointed Alonso de la Capella as a judge in 1705. He died in 1712. Military tribunals dealt with criminal cases for the civil population as well as the garrison, and this procedure continued until the middle of the eighteenth century.

The first Charter of Justice, granted by George I in 1720, established a court of summary jurisdiction for personal suits, and a judge named John Beaver was appointed to preside over it. The charter stated that the law applicable was to be the law of Spain, a curious ruling when one considers that nearly all the Spanish population had left in 1704. However, it did perhaps provide some continuity in the law for those civilians, mostly of Genoese ancestry, who remained, for they had lived under Spanish law before 1704.

In 1740 there was a second charter, granted by George II, which was not promulgated in Gibraltar but was held by the Privy Council to apply. It contained the words 'We will that the laws of England be the measure of justice between the parties', apparently pointing to a sudden change of attitude, but it may have been induced by what was happening in practice. Judges trained in English law would have tended to be guided by its principles even in applying Spanish law, but information is lacking on judgments delivered at the time.

In 1752 there was another charter, which established the first justices of the peace. This was revoked in 1817 by a fourth charter, which superseded all previous charters and established a Small Debts Court, a Court of Civil Pleas, a Court of General Sessions (with almost unlimited criminal jurisdiction), a Court of Quarter Sessions, the Assize of Bread (concerned with the quality and the price) and a Court of Appeal. For a population of about 12,000 Gibraltar was thus heavily endowed with courts. Judicial officers tended to proliferate, too. Among them was one known as the judge advocate who sat from time to time on almost any court dealing with any subject; he was the representative of the governor, who was the head of all courts until 1830.

The situation was rationalised in 1830 when a civil magistrate was appointed and a fifth Charter of Justice established a Supreme Court. The judge advocate disappeared, and the judge presiding over the Supreme Court became head of the judiciary. The judge became known as chief justice after Sir James Cochrane had been appointed in 1841. Sir James had a long career in high judicial office, as he was appointed attorney general in 1830 before becoming head of the judiciary, a post in which he remained until 1877.

Independently of the charters, Admiralty jurisdiction was established in 1739 through a Vice-Admiral's Court, which assumed particular importance in prize cases during the Napoleonic Wars. In 1872 it heard the well known case of the *Mary Celeste*, which was found drifting unmanned and was brought into Gibraltar by the *Dei Gratia*. The reasons for the abandoning of the *Mary Celeste* have never been satisfactorily established, as the ship was in good order, the sails were set, and there was plenty of food and water on board. There has been much speculation, but the evidence before the court left the mystery unsolved.

### ENGLISH-STYLE COURTS AND LAW

Since 1830 the courts have been closely related in style and practice to the English courts. Under the Gibraltar Constitution Order 1969 the courts comprise the Court of Appeal, the Supreme Court, the Court of First Instance and the Magistrate's Court. The Court of Appeal does not conduct much business, but there is a right of further appeal to the Judicial Committee of the Privy Council; this puts ultimate judicial control in a body composed largely of the Law Lords, who sit when the House of Lords exercises its appellate jurisdiction over the English courts.

The chief justice presides over the Supreme Court, which exercises jurisdiction similar to all the Divisions of the High Court in England and the Crown Courts. The Supreme Court holds four sessions annually for criminal trials and appeals. The chief justice sits with a jury for criminal trials, and proceedings are similar to those in Crown Courts in England, except that there are only nine jurymen. The Supreme Court hears appeals from the Court of First Instance and the Magistrate's Court, which courts correspond respectively to County Courts and Magistrates' Courts in England. The Stipendiary Magistrate normally presides over the Magistrate's Court, but two or more justices of the peace can sit if he is absent.

The charter of 1740 applied the laws of England, but the present position stems from an Order in Council made in 1884, which applied English law as it existed on 31 December 1883, subject to local enactments and to subsequently passed laws of England expressly or by general implication applying to Gibraltar. Since 1962 there has been an ordinance incorporated in the laws of Gibraltar (Cap 5) which applies common law and equity from time to time in force and specifies certain United Kingdom Acts applicable to Gibraltar. In practice statute law is now largely based on ordinances passed in Gibraltar. A large body of law is, however, based upon English common law and equity, and as in England this has not been codified; much of the law of contract and tort falls into this category. New legislation in England is normally followed by similar legislation in Gibraltar. In 1972, for example, an ordinance was passed abolishing actions for breach of promise of marriage, enticement and claims for damages for adultery, as had been done in England.

## COMPARISON WITH SPANISH LAW

Any change in Gibraltar's status giving sovereignty to Spain would require close examination from the point of view of public and personal law. It has been suggested by Spain that Gibraltarians should continue under their own civil laws and local government. This might seem practicable from a Spanish point of view, as there are many local variations in laws in Spain – Catalan law, for example, is composed of elements of Catalan civil law and the canon law, as well as the universal provisions of the Civil Code. There is, however, a fundamental difference between English law and Spanish law in the very existence of a Civil Code in Spain with a background of Roman law. English law is based upon judicial precedent in the development of the common law and equity over centuries of time.

### GIBRALTAR HOUSE OF ASSEMBLY

The steps taken towards some form of responsible government between the world wars and after World War II have already been mentioned. The former home of the Exchange Committee now accommodates the Gibraltar House of Assembly. This is a fitting use for the Exchange Building standing on Main Street at the entrance to the Piazza, for it was from here that it became customary in the nineteenth century for the Exchange Committee to make representations regarding various matters, particularly ones connected with trade and taxation. The City Hall at the opposite end of the Piazza housed the City Council from 1924 until 1969, and it is still used as government offices, although the Council was abolished by the Gibraltar Constitution Order in Council of 1969. This Order also provided for the Legislative Council to be replaced by the Gibraltar House of Assembly, which consists of a Speaker and fifteen elected members, together with the Attorney General and the Financial and Development Secretary as ex-officio members. The Order did not give any original or casting vote to the Speaker, and on a motion putting confidence in the government in issue neither of the ex-officio members was allowed to vote by the Order.

Executive authority remained vested in the governor, but a Gibraltar Council composed of five of the elected members of the Assembly and four ex-officio members was set up. A Council of Ministers constituted by the chief minister and not more than eight or less than four other ministers was also formed. The Order required the governor to act in accordance with the advice of the Council of Ministers on defined domestic matters, but empowered him to consult the Gibraltar Council, and provided for some powers of disallowance of laws. There was a long list of defined domestic matters in the Order under the main headings of Municipal Services, Social Services, Revenue Contributing Services, Public Services and Personal Status.

In practice the Council of Ministers became the government in respect of defined domestic matters, with ministers responsible for such departments as Health, Labour and Education. Defence, external affairs and internal security remained reserved to the governor, as well as responsibility for the civil service and the appointment of judges.

### THE PUBLIC SERVICES

The governor is assisted by a deputy governor, who is the head of the secretariat. This also forms the link with government departments and bodies such as the Police Force, organised under the Commissioner of Police on a pattern closely related to that of similar forces in the United Kingdom. Its strength is only about 200 men and women for all municipal duties, including traffic regulation, as well as some dockyard security and immigration work, so a high degree of efficiency is required. Basic training takes place in Gibraltar, but it is followed whenever possible by training in Britain.

The other public services, including housing, social security, welfare and fire-fighting services (as well as health and education, which have already been mentioned), are British in style. From a local government point of view there are similarities to an English county council. The functions are, however, centralised in a city state without the delegation of municipal matters to a subordinate council.

About a quarter of the revenue required to finance government services comes from import duties. For a long time the list of dutiable goods was confined to wines, malted liquors, spirits and tobacco, but since 1955 there has been a steadily increasing list. There are *ad valorem* duties on manufactured goods, and there is an export duty on fuel oil.

The rates of income tax and estate duty are substantially lower than in the United Kingdom, and there is a maximum rate of estate duty of 20 per cent, so that in some respects Gibraltar might be regarded as a rich man's paradise, at least in his latter days. It is not, however, easy to establish a domicile, for various reasons, including a shortage of accommodation. For Gibraltarians there are substantial fiscal advantages in being associated with the United Kingdom without being integrated with it. All forms of taxation are lower, but the cost of many essential commodities is higher and the ways of earning a living are much more limited.

Gibraltar was temporarily excluded from the sterling area in 1972, but it returned again on joining the European Economic Community with Britain on 1 January 1973. British banking practices are followed, and United Kingdom currency circulates as well as Gibraltar currency. There are a number of international banks situated in Main Street.

### THE POLITICAL SCENE

The constitution that came into force in 1969 protected Gibraltarians from passing under any other sovereignty 'against their freely and democratically expressed wishes'. There was formerly a strong Integration with Britain Party, which favoured closer ties. This party formed the first government, led by Major Peliza, under the 1969 constitution, with the aid of three independents – the Isola brothers and Major Gache. In 1972 Sir Joshua Hassan returned to the leadership of the government with the combined Labour Party and Association for the Advancement of Civil Rights. This party gained eight out of the fifteen seats, after having held seven in the previous assembly. Sir Joshua's party favours the maintenance of the present status of Gibraltar, and it was returned again in 1976 with a majority of one.

# 9      COMMUNICATIONS AND COMMERCE

I N TIMES of peace and trade as well as during periods of war and siege sea communications are Gibraltar's life-line. Air transport has become the principal means of travel for passengers, but the great bulk of Gibraltar's needs are still imported by sea. Industrial work in Gibraltar mainly consists of building construction, servicing naval ships, merchant-ship repairs and bottling beer and mineral waters; and the materials required for these industries, even including sand for building, are imported by sea, together with vehicles, machinery, clothing and household needs. There is no agricultural production, apart from a little vegetable-growing, so that most of Gibraltar's food supply is imported by sea, though air transport is used for some fresh and frozen foods. When the Spanish frontier was open, most of the fresh food came in from Spain, but there have always been some supplies from Morocco, and this source has been developed further in recent years. A total quantity of about 350,000 tons of goods and food supplies comes in through the port each year, fuel oils and lubricants accounting for about a third of this total.

### COMMERCIAL PORT AND NAVAL HARBOUR

As well as providing an entry for imports, the naval harbour and commercial port are one of Gibraltar's main sources of livelihood. There is a large re-export of supplies to merchant ships, among which fuel oil accounts for about 90 per cent of Gibraltar's exports by value. In addition to oil, ships are supplied with food and water and a variety of other needs, including pilotage and medical services. The port medical services have a long-established reputation for efficiency, which is particularly useful for British ships, as there are no language problems.

The closure of the Suez Canal in 1967 caused a reduction in the number of ships using Gibraltar, and there was a decline in shipping tonnage using the port from over 13 million tons in 1966 to just under 10 million in 1970; but by 1972 there had been a recovery to the former figure. The reopening of the canal has changed the pattern again, and put Gibraltar back on the Mediterranean sea route to the Far East.

During the two world wars and the intervening period the commercial port consisted of an anchorage in the bay and Waterport Wharf, situated to the north of the much longer North Mole. Only small ships could tie up at the Wharf, so that most cargoes were unloaded into lighters in the bay. The naval harbour was only used by warships, troopships and fleet auxiliaries. Now merchant ships can tie up on the western arm of the North Mole, both inside and outside the naval harbour, and the old destroyer pens running south-wards into the harbour – now called Jetties 1, 2 and 3 – are also used for commercial operations. There are 5,500ft (1,678·2m) of alongside berthing available in the north-eastern portion of the harbour, which includes part of the Detached Mole. Many merchant ships still anchor in the bay, particularly when they are not carrying out a large amount of unloading or taking on oil, as this is more economical. Various grades of fuel oil are available at all the alongside berths, except those on the Detached Mole; modern blending and metering methods are used and oil can be supplied at a rate of up to 250 tons (254 tonnes) an hour.

There are three drydocks at the southern end of the naval harbour, with a total length of 2,104ft (641·3m). The largest, Prince of Wales Dock, which is over 900ft (274·32m) long, could accommodate the battleships of former times, but only much smaller ships now normally use these docks. The dry-dock area covers 11 acres (4·45 hectares) of the 440 acres (178·2 hectares) enclosed within the moles. Subject to naval requirements the drydock facilities can now be used by merchant ships. There is also a commercial ship-repair yard situated outside the harbour to the north of the western end of the airport runway.

As well as large ocean-going vessels, many small craft visit Gibraltar and use the small-craft anchorage situated between Waterport Wharf and the airport runway. There is also a yacht marina in this area, with a quay frontage of 300ft (91·44m), which provides servicing for yachts and small craft. Waterport Wharf itself is used for offloading goods that have been discharged into lighters, and for the Bland Line service to Tangier. Facilities on this crossing of the Straits include a car ferry.

Other services to ships provided by Gibraltar are those of the port signal station and the Europa lighthouse. The latter, which was completed in 1838, stands 61ft (18·59m) above the ground and 156ft (47·55m) above sea level, provides a beam that can be seen for 30 miles (48·28km) in clear weather, and is equipped with a fog signal.

### AIR TRAFFIC

The main features of the airport have already been described. Strong winds can cause problems for aircraft, but the airport rarely has to be closed to traffic. There are direct flights by British Airways between London and Gibraltar, with connecting flights within the United Kingdom. Flights to Tangier are provided twice daily by Gibair, and Gibraltar is used as a staging post for tourists going to Morocco. Holiday arrangements are made by tour operators to provide for part of the time being spent in Morocco at places such as Tangier, Fez, Marrakesh and Agadir, and it is also possible for excursions to be made to Gibraltar in the course of a Moroccan holiday.

As well as being used for passenger traffic, the airport provides for cargo services, and there are some exclusively cargo flights, particularly for frozen food from the United Kingdom. The RAF still uses the airport, but the total number of both civil and RAF flights taking place during a day can easily be handled. The runway of 2,000yd (1,828·8m) length is not adequate for the largest Trident aircraft in use by British Airways carrying a full load. This reduces the profitability of Gibraltar flights, so extension of the runway is necessary. Problems arose from Spanish restrictions on flying over Spanish air space in the vicinity of the Rock, but these have been overcome by the routing system now used.

### POSTS, TELECOMMUNICATIONS AND BROADCASTING

Mail travels to London and Tangier by the direct airline flights. Gibraltar's stamps have a history of over 100 years, and in 1931 one of the first pictorial issues by a British colony was produced. It gave a view of the Rock. There have been many subsequent pictorial stamps, including some of such ships as the *Victory*, the *Mary Celeste*, the *Hood* and the *Ark Royal*. The interest of philatelists in these stamps provides a little revenue.

There are over 7,000 telephones in Gibraltar and over 6,000 television sets. Although telephone communications with Spain were cut in 1969, there are efficient services by other routes to the United Kingdom and other parts of the world. Television services are operated by Radio Gibraltar, which provides about 16 hours of sound radio each day and between 4 and 8 hours of television.

### ROADS

Roads cover a total of 26 miles (41·84km) in Gibraltar, including $\frac{3}{4}$ mile (1·21km) of tunnels that are open to the public. On the eastern side a tunnel, open at weekends only, allows one to make a complete circuit of the Rock by road. There are also over 4 miles (6·44km) of pedestrian paths, including steps up the steep slopes of the Rock.

Walking provides the best means of seeing things in Gibraltar, but it is strenuous, particularly in warm weather, as there is nearly always a hill to climb. There is plenty of motor transport – over 5,500 cars and taxis and about 500 commercial vehicles. Taxis are readily available, with helpful and cheerful drivers who will quote a price of a journey and keep to it.

It is perhaps surprising that there are so many cars for use in such a small area now that there is no road communication with Spain. After the frontier was closed to vehicles in 1966, there was a decline in the number registered in Gibraltar for a few years, but now there are 10 per cent more than there were before the closure. For a small place Gibraltar is well supplied with private cars, and they make travelling much easier in a place without much level ground.

## THE TRADE BALANCE AND THE TOURIST INDUSTRY

Re-exports cover the cost of less than half Gibraltar's imports. On the credit side, in addition to re-exports and services to ships, there are goods and services supplied to the garrison and naval establishments, the tourist industry and development aid from the United Kingdom. The last of these items has amounted on average to about £2 million per annum in direct grants and loans since 1970. Over half the development aid is spent on housing, and Gibraltar contributes about a quarter of the cost of the various projects from its own budget. Since the end of World War II over 3,000 new dwellings, nearly all flats, have been completed, mostly in new estates; among these the Laguna, the Glacis and the Varyl Begg outside the northern boundaries of the town are the most impressive. In 1939 Gibraltar was one of the most overcrowded places in Europe with about half its families living in only one room and poor amenities in some of the old buildings in the town. It might, therefore, be said that Gibraltar was overdue for some aid from the United Kingdom, particularly as the overcrowded state of the town was at least partly the result of much land outside being the preserve of the services.

The pattern of tourism has changed considerably since the frontier with Spain was closed to vehicles in 1966. The total number of visitors to Gibraltar reached a peak figure of

738,000 in 1964, when many tourists combined a visit to Gibraltar with a holiday in Southern Spain, and this pattern continued to some extent until the Algeciras ferry was closed in 1969. In recent years between 30,000 and 40,000 tourists have stayed in hotels for an average of about a week, and about another 100,000 have visited Gibraltar from cruising liners or small craft, or on day trips from Morocco. Much government effort goes into encouraging tourism, although all the hotels in Gibraltar are privately owned.

### THE HOTELS

Tour operators quote an inclusive price for travel and accommodation, and their activities are mainly based on eight hotels. On the eastern side of the Rock there are two modern hotels – the Caleta Palace and Both Worlds. The hotels have easy access to the beaches of Catalan Bay and Sandy Bay, and the Caleta Palace has its own swimming pool. It is operated as a catering hotel, but Both Worlds consists of self-catering flats, with a central restaurant and a number of bars for those who do not wish to cater for themselves, or wish to meet friends. Both hotels provide good facilities for family holidays based on beaches. In the hottest weather some shade from the shadow of the Rock in the late afternoon is an advantage, and the east side does not suffer from the overhanging Levanter cloud when the wind is in the east. There is a disadvantage in the hotels being situated about 2 miles (3·22km) from the town, but there is a frequent bus service and taxis can be obtained quite easily.

On the western side the Rock Hotel is perhaps the best known. It was in operation for about 6 years before World War II and at that time it was unrivalled in its amenities and comfort. It has its own gardens, and also enjoys an excellent view across the Alameda Gardens to the harbour and across the bay to the hills west of Algeciras. Like all hotels, The Rock caters for families of all ages, but it is perhaps more suitable for visitors who wish to see as much as possible of Gibraltar, rather than simply to enjoy sunshine on the beaches. The Rock Hotel is only a short distance from the town, but the climb up the hill just outside Southport Gates is quite a steep one.

Among the hotels in the town the Bristol, situated in Cathedral Square between Main Street and the Line Wall, deserves special mention. The oldest part of the building dates from 1865, and an extension was built on the corner of Cathedral Square and Bomb House Lane in 1874. A small hotel was opened in 1890, and it has belonged to and been managed by the Piccone family until the present day. For a long time the hotel catered largely for families of naval officers and members of the garrison. It has been extensively modernised since World War II, and it now provides a visitor with a central position in a comparatively quiet area of the town. The hotel owns a garden with a small swimming pool in it on the opposite side of Bomb House Lane.

The most modern hotel in the town is the Holiday Inn, which opened in 1973 in Governor's Parade, opposite the Garrison Library. It is a contrast in style with the older buildings in the area, for it is of tall modern construction with accommodation for about 200 people. There is a roof area, with facilities for relaxing in the sunshine and a swimming pool, from which excellent views can be obtained – towards the Rock, old and modern houses rising in tiers, together with Moorish Castle and many other fortifications; and seawards, the panorama of the harbour.

Other hotels in the town include the Victoria and the Montarik. The latter consists partly of the buildings that composed the Grand Hotel, which like the Bristol was one of the older hotels in the town. Just outside Southport Gates stands the Queen's Hotel, which is conveniently situated on bus routes just north of the Alameda Gardens. Altogether the hotels mentioned provide accommodation for about 1,700 people. The hotel industry suffered a serious setback when Spanish staff were no longer able to cross the frontier, as services had been largely dependent upon such staff. New staff were, however, recruited from Morocco, and the standards of service provided have been steadily built up again. Moroccans had difficulty with the English language when they first arrived, but they were very willing to learn whatever was required of them and they have overcome their language difficulties; those who come from Moroccan towns such as Fez and Rabat, which were formerly in French Morocco, speak French fluently.

During the summer months the hotels are usually full, but there is scope for expansion of the tourist industry in winter. Sunshine is not assured, as in summer, but the weather is warmer than it is in Britain, and the winter is a good time of the year for walking and seeing the many things of historic interest in Gibraltar.

# AROUND THE ROCK

THERE are five beaches around the Rock for visitors who want to find sunshine and sea bathing. On the western side Little Bay and Camp Bay in the Europa area have been equipped with changing facilities and safe pools for children. On the eastern side there is more space on the sandy shores of Sandy Bay, Catalan Bay and Eastern Beach. The village of Catalan Bay is well worth visiting, too, as the only settlement on the eastern side.

A tour arranged by one of the travel agencies can give a general idea of the places to be visited. There are plenty of these tours, and it is a good plan to find one, starting in the town, which includes Moorish Castle, the Upper Rock and Europa Point. By taking such a tour soon after arriving in Gibraltar a visitor can decide where he wishes to spend most of his time. He will be able to compare, for example, the Upper Rock with its trees, flowering plants and bird life, with the closely populated and busy town, which can best be seen on foot.

### A WALK AROUND TOWN

A walk up Main Street is well worth while for anyone making either a short or longer visit to Gibraltar. The walk can begin at the northern end of the town at Casemates Gates, which were the point of entry for many people coming ashore at Waterport Wharf during the nineteenth and twentieth centuries. The gates stand on the site of an old watergate that existed when the sea came up to this point. The arches constituting the entrances for traffic to Casemates Square were opened in 1824 and 1883; the inscription above the earlier arch refers to the governorship of the Earl of Chatham, a successor of Pitt the Elder, and the later arch refers to General Adye. The Grand Casemates inside the square, which held stores for former garrisons, carry an inscription of 1817 referring to Sir George Don, lieutenant-governor between 1814 and 1832.

At the north-east corner of the square an archway leads to the old Landport Gate, which still stands in the style of its reconstruction after the siege of 1727, when a Spanish bombardment did much damage in the Casemates Square area. On the west side of the square the modern Department of Health building contrasts with the older solid stone construction of the Grand Casemates. Upwards towards the Rock the scene is dominated by the keep of Moorish Castle, and an interesting feature to look for is the way in which houses have been built in rows rising one above the other.

Main Street itself may be reached via the southern end of Casemates Square. The street is a narrow one about ¾ mile (1·21km) long, which forms the main commercial artery of the town. Even narrower streets run off to the east, where they slope steeply up the rock, and to the west, where there is a much more gentle slope towards the Line Wall, which stands above the naval harbour. These narrow streets have such English names as Turnbull's Lane, Engineer Lane, Parliament Lane and Bedlam Court, but most of the names on the shops and commercial houses are Gibraltarian, such as Galliano, Bassadone and Stagnetto. There are also some Indian names, such as Chellaram and Dialdas, to be seen on some shops, particularly at the northern end of Main Street. The shops here began to flourish between the world wars through being well placed for visitors coming off ships into the town.

The Exchange Building stands about half-way along Main Street at the centre of the town. As well as accommodating the Gibraltar Assembly on the first floor, it provides a centre for tourist information and a place for refreshments at street level. Taking a seat outside the building gives one a good point for observing the Main Street scene. It is a busy street, but there is not the same bustling and jostling as there is

129

in the more northern parts of Europe. There is time for the courtesies of life, which Gibraltarians give in very good measure, and for a drink and a chat.

Just opposite the Exchange Building there is often an Indian awaiting custom outside his shop, a sight reminiscent of Bombay. People passing sometimes include servicemen in uniform, but more often they are to be seen in the town in mufti enjoying their leisure hours. Their families may also be in evidence on shopping expeditions, with pushchairs for children, who might well be seen in any English town. In contrast to the lightly clad British housewives from a more northern climate, the older generation of Gibraltarian women wear black clothing in southern Spanish style. Even more heavily clad are some Moroccan women, with their faces covered with the yashmak; and some Moroccan men wear long Moorish-style robes, particularly when the weather becomes a little colder in winter. The scene varies according to the season and the time of day. In the morning there is a slow start to the activities of Main Street, unless a cruising ship happens to have come into port. There is a gradual increase in activity as the morning goes on, but at 1.00pm there is a sudden closing down of shops and most businesses for two hours or so in accordance with the Spanish and Mediterranean custom of taking a siesta in the middle of the day. The afternoon's business also begins slowly, but there is no hurry to close in the evening, and business in some shops continues for long after dark.

A little way up Main Street from the Exchange Building stands the Roman Catholic Cathedral of St Mary the Crowned, on the site of an old Moorish Mosque, which was converted to a church after the Moors had been finally expelled in 1462. Many changes have been made, but parts of the building date back to the early Spanish days. Like most other buildings in the town it required much restoration after the Great Siege of 1779–83.

The Anglican Cathedral of the Holy Trinity lies a little further south, just off Main Street in Cathedral Square. It is one of the many developments of Sir George Don's time,-

like the Law Courts standing a little further along Main Street. The Cathedral was built when King's Chapel, the garrison church, became too small to accommodate civilians on Sundays. The Chapel is about another hundred yards from the Law Courts, next to the Convent of which it originally formed a part. The term 'convent' is perhaps confusing, in giving the idea that the building was a nunnery; it was in fact occupied by Franciscan friars who left when the British arrived. The remainder of the building, apart from King's Chapel, now constitutes the Governor's residence. It was known as Government House between 1908 and 1943, its name being changed on the orders of King Edward VII in 1908 on the grounds that the word Convent was inappropriate for a governor's residence; but his grandson King George VI, after a visit in 1943 on the way to see his troops in North Africa, ordered the historical name to be restored.

There is a weekly ceremonial changing of the guard outside the Convent with the governor in attendance on the balcony. This is performed in the usual British army style, preceded by a march down part of Main Street, though individual regiments bring their own particular customs into the ceremony. Another parade much more particularly related to Gibraltar is the Ceremony of the Keys, which occasionally takes place in Casemates Square. It commemorates the ancient custom of locking up the fortress at Landport Gate at night. Some governors were reputed to keep the keys under their pillows in the Convent when the guard had handed them over each night.

From the Convent onwards to Southport Gates Main Street widens and becomes perhaps less interesting. There are a few more shops, some old army quarters, John Mackintosh Hall and Ince's Hall, which has a theatre and provides other recreational activities for the garrison. John Mackintosh Hall is the most impressive building in this part of the town, open to the public and well worth visiting. The southern entrance to the town is by Southport Gates, which go through Charles V Wall. The original arch has the Spanish royal arms above it, and a second arch, made in 1883, carries the British lion and unicorn above it together with the coats of arms of Gibraltar and of General Sir John Adye, who was governor at the time the arch was opened. A third gate was made in 1967.

Beyond Charles V Wall there was a moat, part of which is now occupied by the Trafalgar Cemetery – a beautiful garden of remembrance, particularly in spring. Other naval battles commemorated as well as Trafalgar include those of Algeciras in 1801, Cadiz in 1810 and Malaga in 1812. The road round the cemetery enters the town again by Prince Edward's Gate, which was cut through Charles V Wall in 1790; it was named after the fourth son of George III, who was serving as a young officer in the garrison at the time, and became governor as the Duke of Kent in 1802. Just outside the wall, near where the gate now stands, lay the old Spanish Bastion of Santiago, which was built in 1552 as part of the defences against pirates, like the wall itself. The British later gave the bastion the much less impressive name of Flat Bastion.

A walk northwards along Prince Edward Road passes mixed Spanish and British style buildings, some of which stand on solid masses of limestone; the road is a narrow one and it is cut into the Rock in places. Forty Steps, opposite Gowlands Ramp going up the Rock, leads down to Town Range, which runs parallel to Main Street and contains some of the oldest army buildings, dating from the eighteenth century. There are some interesting old inscriptions on these buildings: the house opposite the steps was once designated Officers' Barracks No I, but the house in Georgian style at the bottom of the steps has the more impressive name of Officers' Quarters No II. Town Range has a number of buildings in similar style along it on the way northwards to Governor's Parade, which was once an open space used for military ceremonies. Most of the buildings in Governor's Parade date from the nineteenth century. The area constitutes a square, with the stone-built Presbyterian Church of Scotland standing at the southern end and providing a reminder of its native land.

The Garrison Library dominates the scene on the eastern

side of Governor's Parade, although it is now dwarfed by the Holiday Inn on the western side. The idea of establishing a library was one that interested the writer Captain John Drinkwater after the Great Siege of 1779–83, and one was started in temporary premises. In 1793 a committee was formed with the idea of establishing a library building. The committee received the encouraging information in 1799 that 'Mr Pitt will lose no time in authorising its execution'. Prince Frederick, the Duke of York, had assisted in obtaining the Prime Minister's interest as a means of saving the members of the garrison from 'having their minds enervated and vitiated by dissipation' – a possibility envisaged by the committee. The building was completed in 1804, and the library now has a large collection of old and modern books, including some about Gibraltar unobtainable elsewhere. It welcomes temporary members who are visiting Gibraltar and are interested in using its facilities.

Other nineteenth-century buildings in Governor's Parade include the Sergeants' Mess and the Theatre Royal. The latter was opened in 1847, but it now has a sad neglected appearance behind an early Victorian front. It has prospered at times, but it is now closed owing to lack of support, like many similar small theatres in Britain.

There are a number of streets leading out of Governor's Parade, including Library Ramp, which goes up the Rock along one of the old routes used for hauling up supplies. Governor's Street, like Town Range, continues parallel to Main Street, and there is a route back to Main Street by way of City Mill Lane from Governor's Street. This lane is typical of the many little streets off Main Street, which contain small shops selling groceries and many household requirements that still survive in spite of the development of some supermarkets in Main Street. City Mill Lane also has a night club in it near its exit into Main Street – opposite the entrance to John Mackintosh Square, which stands behind the Exchange Building. The area around the square has been a centre of activity since the Spanish days in Gibraltar. In early British times it was occupied by the garrison, and the square contained a guard room and a whipping post, but later commerce and government took over from the military, who moved away from the town. Since World War II a Spanish-style piazza has been laid out in the middle of the square, which was formerly known as Commercial Square. Between the world wars the central part of the square contained the Jews Market, composed of an untidy assortment of stalls selling antiques, objets d'art and many other things.

The City Hall stands on the west side of the square. It began as Aaron Cardozo's mansion, when the building was completed in 1815, but became the Garrison Club in 1833 and the Club House Hotel in 1839. It continued as a hotel until 1875, when it was sold to the Larios family. In 1876, after it had been converted back into a private residence, it was occupied by the Duke of Connaught, the third son of Queen Victoria, and became known as Connaught House. The mansion was only a royal residence for a few months, but it continued as a home of the Larios family until 1920, when it was sold to the government. It became the City Hall in 1924 and served as such until the Council ceased to exist in 1969, but the building continues to be used for government offices.

A narrow street running northwards from John Mackintosh Square is known as Irish Town, and by following it past the Police Station a few yards from the square, and along its length to Cooperage Lane, one may return to Main Street at the entrance to Casemates Square. This completes a figure of eight type of walk around the town. The origin of the name Irish Town is obscure, but it is now the area containing shipping and other commercial offices. Cooperage Lane provides a reminder of an industry that flourished in the days of the Dukes of Medina before the Spanish Crown finally took Gibraltar into its possession in 1502.

### WALKS OUTSIDE THE TOWN

All places of interest in Gibraltar can be visited on foot from the town, but some walking up steep hills is necessary, so it is often better to go by bus or taxi to a selected point and walk from there. In the immediate vicinity of the town a walk through Landport Gate from Casemates Square leads to some interesting old defensive sites. On the left-hand side outside the gate lies the old Grand Battery, and on the other side the old defences of King's Lines and Queen's Lines, beginning with Hesse's Demi-Bastion, which now houses the water-supply pumping station. Many of the old defences are now hidden behind the Laguna Housing Estate, but some can still be seen when walking through the estate; Prince's Lines higher up the Rock are much more clearly visible. A return to the town along Smith-Dorrien Avenue to Line Wall Road gives one some idea of the old Line Wall defences, but a better impression can be gained by going on another walk outside the town through Casemates Gates. This walk leads to reclaimed land, and a view of the defences from below, as they presented themselves to the sea. There are some nineteenth-century fortifications, such as the West Place of Arms just outside the gates, and walking along Queensway allows one to observe the old Line Wall. It includes Montagu Bastion, Orange Bastion, King's Bastion and South Bastion, which all played a part in setting the Spanish floating batteries on fire during the Great Siege.

At the southern end of Queensway just beyond South Bastion the road turns eastwards near the entrance to the naval dockyard, and passes through Ragged Staff Gates, which stand near the site of an old wharf used in both Spanish and British days. The name is thought to refer to the staff that marked the point for ships. The road beyond the gates leads up to Southport Gates, so that the walk can be completed by entering Main Street at this point.

Another walk outside the town beginning at Southport Gates can be taken up Europa Road as far as the Rock Hotel. From here a leisurely stroll can be made after the steep climb through the many little paths of the Alameda Gardens down to Rosia Road, which provides a route back to the town. By the side of the road there is a wide promenade passing along the top of some more old seaward defences, including

Jumper's Bastion. It is an area in which the British and Dutch forces gained a foothold soon after landing in 1704.

The Waterworks and Moorish Castle can be reached by means of a steep climb up steps and narrow lanes from Casemates Square. It is, however, only possible to see inside the Waterworks on a conducted tour, for which transport is arranged, and when visiting Moorish Castle on foot it is a little less strenuous to walk up the more gentle slopes of Library Ramp, Prince Edward's Road, Castle Road and Willis's Road.

### MOORISH CASTLE

The term Moorish Castle is now often used when referring to the tower that formed the keep of the Castle, and this is the outstanding feature still to be seen. The tower is open to visitors, and climbing it gives both an excellent idea of its solid construction and finally a view all around from the top. The thick solid walls, which withstood the cannon fire of sieges, are built of a conglomerate of stones, cement and clay. From the top of the tower a view down towards Casemates Square overlooks the area at one time occupied by the Moorish Castle, now covered by later fortifications, such as the British Grand Battery, and by the many buildings rising in tiers up the Rock. It is, however, possible to envisage the area covered by the Castle, and to see how it presented a formidable defence to the north of the Rock in the days when the defenders could send down arrows from longbows on to troops advancing to the attack with battering rams. A look southwards towards Europa and eastwards up the Rock discloses the weakness of the Castle in that it could be outflanked and attacked from above after a landing from the sea. At the time of the attack of Alfonso XI in 1333 the castle was even more vulnerable, as the present tower did not exist, although there was a less substantial one on or near the same site. The unsuccessful attack induced the Moors to build most of the works that can be seen today, before Alfonso's next attack in 1349. Some improvements and renovations had been made in the Castle area before the successful Spanish attack of 1462, but there were no great changes in the general nature of the fortifications which ran down to the sea west of Casemates Square.

The defence of the tower by the Spanish governor Esteban de Villacreces is worth remembering, as he spent five months inside the keep before surrendering to Henry de Guzman, the Duke of Medina Sidonia, in 1467. This was the last great episode in the history of the Castle itself, but it served as a refuge against the Turkish pirates in 1540, and continued to play a part in the history of Gibraltar as a whole.

A walk down past the gatehouse by way of many steps and narrow lanes to Casemates Square gives one an opportunity to see small sections of old walls. These give some idea of the general nature of the old castle, which was so much bigger than the small area around the keep. A look upwards at the keep at night when it is floodlit in summer gives a good idea of its majesty against the background of the limestone of the Rock.

### THE UPPER ROCK

Most of the main features of the Upper Rock have already been described. A tour by road gives a good general idea of the area, but some walking is necessary to study its interesting features. There are plenty of places to sit and rest at intervals, and while doing so it is interesting to consider how the gunners in former days used the large rings attached to the Rock in places to haul up their guns. A walk of 4–5 miles (6·44–8·05km) covers the ground from the town up the Rock and back. There is a good route through the Alameda Gardens, up Engineer Road and along Queen's Road, which runs a few hundred feet below the summit of the Rock before returning to the town down Willis's Road, or by one of the footpaths that can be found fairly easily. There is one going down near Devil's Gap Battery that shortens the walk and provides a view of a World War I and II British 6in (15·24cm) gun site, with the guns still in position.

The cable-car service provides a very good way of visiting

the Upper Rock, as the station at the top is at the middle of the Upper Rock at a point once occupied by a signal station. There are fine views both to the east and the west, and walks from there run mostly down hill. St Michael's Cave is a few hundred yards away to the south. The route to it is near the line taken by the party of 500 men who spent a night in the cave in November 1704, after coming up the goatherd's path on the eastern side of the Rock during the twelfth siege designed to recapture Gibraltar from the British. A walk on from St Michael's Cave to Jews Gate runs through a good area for the study of the natural vegetation and bird life of the Upper Rock, and there are plenty of small paths that can be followed. Only a few well marked areas of the Upper Rock are restricted for British Ministry of Defence purposes, so it is possible to wander freely.

A walk northwards from St Michael's Cave along Queen's Road and then Old Queen's Road, which is a little lower down the Rock, leads to Charles V Wall and the ruins of the Old Moorish Wall. While the former commands a better field of fire, the latter has a commanding position at its lower end above the Red Sands now occupied by the Alameda Gardens. This area was of great strategic importance in Moorish times. The wall, dating from the twelfth century, lost some of its value after a sea wall was built before the Count of Niebla's attack in 1436.

There is a cable-car station between the two walls at Apes Den. The apes are frequently to be seen in this area, which is used for feeding them, but they roam freely around the Upper Rock. The cable car provides a convenient way back to the town if a visit is to be made to the northern end of the Upper Rock on a separate occasion. Going northwards, Queen's Road leads to some of the sites of the British batteries that formed Willis's Lines at the time of the Great Siege, and also to the Galleries. A walk through the Galleries to St George's Hall shows the field of fire General Eliott wished to cover from the Notch just above St George's Hall. The Notch itself can best be seen from Devil's Tower Road, from where mountaineers can contemplate the climb that has been made up the north face of the Rock, using the Notch as a place to bivouac.

The Galleries now lead right through the Rock to the eastern side, and there is a good view out into the Mediterranean. Time taken in the northern area of the Upper Rock is well spent, as there are excellent views out over the isthmus, where so much history took place. It is a good plan to spend several days on the different parts of the Upper Rock. There are plenty of places for quiet wandering and considering the eventful history of the area as well as its interesting natural features.

### EUROPA POINT

A bus service runs from the town to Europa Point. The route along Europa Road passes the Naval Hospital, which was originally the Military Hospital when there was a separate Naval Hospital in the Rosia Bay area. The two hospitals have now been combined and the present establishment is under naval control. It was opened in 1904, but the old Naval Hospital, which was converted into married quarters in 1924, was more than 100 years older.

The area around Europa is not particularly attractive. It provides some useful recreation areas for the services but it is frequently windswept. On a clear day there are some excellent views across to North Africa and westwards through the Straits, but the coasts are quite frequently shrouded in mist. It is a good area for bird-watching during the migratory seasons, and there are always plenty of seabirds to be seen off the rocky coast. Some good fishing may be found at a few places off Europa Advance Road, which runs north-east from Europa Flats.

The Europa area has not played much part in Gibraltar's history, but the Shrine of Our Lady of Europa is interesting. The image of the Virgin Mary is a wood carving that was enshrined at the southern end of the Rock after the Moorish kingdom in Spain had been finally overcome with the help of the Duke of Medina, who was the overlord of Gibraltar at the end of the fifteenth century. The image was placed in a shrine that suffered from the pillaging of Turkish pirates in 1540, and an even worse disaster occurred in 1704, when British soldiers not only ransacked the shrine but flung the image on to some rocks and damaged it. Father Romero, who stayed to look after the Roman Catholic Cathedral, recovered the image and sent it to Spain, where it remained until it was returned to Gibraltar in 1864. In the meantime the shrine had been turned into a guard room and later destroyed. In 1866, as a result of the efforts of the Vicar Apostolic, John Scandella, the image was carried in solemn procession through the streets of Gibraltar with a regimental band playing, and enshrined in a chapel in the grounds of the Little Sisters of the Poor at Europa. There was a commemorative stamp to this event in 1966, and in 1968 the image was placed in a shrine made out of the remains of a Moorish mosque at Europa.

The shrine in existence in the sixteenth and seventeenth centuries provided a light for sailors, and it was much venerated by passing ships. The modern lighthouse at Europa now performs the function of providing a powerful beam for ships, and it is quite an impressive tower at the southern end of the Rock. While Europa is not the most southerly point in Europe, it can perhaps claim more grandeur than Tarifa Point.

### THE GIBRALTAR MUSEUM

The opening of the Gibraltar Museum in 1930 was largely the result of the formation of the Gibraltar Society about nine months earlier. The building, situated in Bomb House Lane, was previously Ordnance House and occupied by the officer commanding the Royal Army Ordnance Corps. It is a particularly suitable building for a museum, as it incorporates an old Moorish bath house, which can be seen by visitors. In recent years much effort has been put into developing the various subjects covered by the museum. There are sections dealing with animal life, including birds; a section covering prehistoric man, with models of the Neanderthal skulls; and interesting exhibits connected with the sieges and with naval battles in the vicinity. The museum also contains many old prints and some portraits of governors, including General Eliott. The scale model of the Rock as it was in 1865 is perhaps one of the most impressive exhibits, as well as being historically interesting.

A look around the museum in the early stages of a visit to Gibraltar is helpful in giving an idea of the many things to be seen. It is also useful to make a more careful study of it after having made some expeditions on the Rock.

### EATING AND ENTERTAINMENT

Gibraltar has a large variety of restaurants, offering Italian, Indian and Chinese food, as well as English dishes, and for those who feel at home with it there are plenty of places serving fish and chips. Some of the fish has often come out of the seas around Britain, although there is plenty of good fish in the sea around Gibraltar. There are many English-style taverns and bars – Main Street has fifteen in about fifteen hundred yards – and they are open from the middle of the morning for the rest of the day. There are also night clubs for those who wish to dance until the early hours of the morning, and there is the Casino, which is open on most evenings of the week, for gamblers. For those who prefer a quieter life there are many places where on warm evenings they can sit in the open and watch the world go by or look out to sea. A stroll along the promenade above the Line Wall near King's Bastion gives a good view of the lights of the harbour and those around the bay in Spain. On the eastern side the moon rising out of the Mediterranean is a scene to be viewed from Catalan Bay or the Caleta Palace Hotel, or from a verandah of one of the flats of Both Worlds. There is much that is pleasant and relaxing to do during the evenings, and it is safer to walk in the streets of Gibraltar than it is in many cities of Europe.

### GETTING OFF THE ROCK

As long as the Spanish frontier remains closed, the only day excursion outside Gibraltar is a visit to Tangier. This can be made by air or by sea. The latter gives the traveller a chance to look at the coasts around the Straits, and on the way back the approach to the Rock gives the same views as many travellers saw in the past on their way east. A visit to Tangier also helps towards appreciating how confined Gibraltarians have been since the Spanish frontier was closed. Economically Gibraltar has survived, but there is still room for development of the tourist industry and perhaps light industries associated with it, such as printing, publishing, brewing and soft drink manufacture.

Tourism is also useful to Gibraltar in widening understanding of the frontier dispute. In Britain there is a need for a better appreciation of injured Spanish pride and Spanish distrust, dating from the letter from King George I, which became known as his promise to return the Rock. In Spain there is a need to understand that Britain cannot give up sovereignty to Gibraltar as long as the Gibraltarians wish to remain British. Future events, however, such as an enlargement of the European community, might provide a means for the problem to be solved.

# APPENDICES

## 1

## SOME NOTABLE DATES

| Date | Event |
|------|-------|
| 711 | Tarik's Moorish forces land without opposition in April, beginning their invasion of Spain. |
| 1160 | Fortification of Gibraltar ordered by Al-Mu'mim. The Moorish Wall dates from about this time. |
| 1309 | *First Siege.* Alonso Perez de Guzman takes Gibraltar after a siege of one month. |
| 1316 | *Second Siege.* Moorish attempt at recapture fails. |
| 1333 | *Third Siege.* Vasco Perez surrenders to Moorish forces after a siege of four months. |
| 1333 | *Fourth Siege.* Alfonso XI tries to recapture the Rock but fails. |
| 1349–50 | *Fifth Siege.* Alfonso XI makes another attempt to drive out the Moors, but the effort ends in his death of plague in March 1350. |
| 1411 | *Sixth Siege.* The Rock taken by forces of the Granadian Moorish kingdom from the kingdom of Fez. |
| 1436 | *Seventh Siege.* Henry de Guzman, Count of Niebla, fails to capture the Rock and is killed in the attempt. |
| 1462 | *Eighth Siege.* Alonso de Arcos initiates an attack and is joined by other Spanish forces before Gibraltar is captured in the name of the Duke of Medina in August. Later in the year the Crown of Spain annexes it, the Duke giving it up under protest. |
| 1466–67 | *Ninth Siege.* Henry de Guzman, son of the Duke of Medina, captures the Rock after a siege of fifteen months. |
| 1502 | Gibraltar placed under the Crown of Spain by Isabella, with agreement of the third Duke of Medina. |

| | |
|---|---|
| 1506 | *Tenth Siege.* Third Duke of Medina imposes a blockade, but abandons it without serious fighting. |
| 1540 | Turkish pirates land and pillage, taking captives away with them. Most of the captives saved by a Spanish naval squadron. |
| 1624 | Philip IV of Spain visits Gibraltar, and sets in progress many improvements to the defences. |
| 1693 | Some ships of a British convoy escorted by Admiral Rooke on the way to Mediterranean ports shelter in Gibraltar after being scattered by a French attack. |
| 1704 | *Eleventh Siege.* British fleet under Admiral Rooke and British and Dutch land forces under Prince George of Hesse capture Gibraltar on 4 August in the name of King Charles III of Spain after an attack lasting a few days. |
| 1704–05 | *Twelfth Siege.* Forces supporting Philip V of Spain begin an attack on the Rock in October 1704. The siege continues until April 1705, but is unsuccessful. |
| 1713 | Spain cedes Gibraltar to Britain by Article X of the Treaty of Utrecht. |
| 1727 | *Thirteenth Siege.* Spanish and French attempt made to recapture Gibraltar by a siege begun in February and lasting about five months before hostilities are suspended. |
| 1779–83 | *Fourteenth Siege.* Spanish and French forces besiege the Rock from June 1779 until February 1783. Relieving fleets arrive in 1780, 1781 and 1782. A sortie is made in November 1781 and a heavy bombardment by besieging forces in September 1782. |
| 1789–1815 | French Revolution, followed by the Napoleonic Wars. After a decline in trade following the French Revolution Gibraltar develops as an entrepôt port for British ships excluded from other European ports. Nelson's victory at Trafalgar in 1805 removes the threat of a siege of Gibraltar. The *Victory*, with Nelson's body on board, comes to Rosia Bay a few days after the battle. |
| 1830 | Fifth Charter of Justice sets up Supreme Court, the first move towards civil government. |
| 1865 | Sanitary Commissioners appointed. |
| 1869 | Suez Canal opened. |
| 1893 | Work begun on South Mole, marking the start of the building of the naval harbour of 440 acres (178 hectares), completed by 1905. |

| | |
|---|---|
| 1914–18 | *World War I.* Gibraltar used for examination for contraband, convoy collection and anti-submarine operations. |
| 1921 | City Council elections held, marking the beginning of moves to representative government. |
| 1936–39 | Spanish Civil War. Nationalist troops from Morocco land at Algeciras and elsewhere in July 1936. War ends in April 1939. |
| 1939–45 | *World War II.* Gibraltar again used for convoy collection and as base for anti-submarine operations. It is main base for the launching of the British and American campaign in North Africa. |
| 1950 | First Legislative Council established. |
| 1954 | Spanish consul withdrawn and restrictions begun on crossing the frontier at La Linea. |
| 1969 | Spanish frontier closes at La Linea and ferry to Algeciras withdrawn. Telephone links with Spain cut. |

## 2

## ARTICLE X OF THE TREATY OF UTRECHT

The Catholic King does hereby, for himself, his heirs and successors, yield to the Crown of Great Britain the full and entire propriety of the town and castle of Gibraltar, together with the port, fortifications and forts thereunto belonging; and he gives up the said propriety to be held and enjoyed absolutely with all manner of right for ever, without any exception or impediment whatsoever. But that abuses and frauds may be avoided by importing any kind of goods, the Catholic King wills and takes it to be understood that the above-named propriety be yielded to Great Britain without any territorial jurisdiction, and without any open communication by land with the country round about. Yet whereas the communication by sea with the coast of Spain may not at all times be safe or open, and thereby it may happen that the garrison and other inhabitants of Gibraltar may be brought to great straits; and as it is the intention of the Catholic King, only that fraudulent importation of goods should, as is above said, be hindered by an inland communication, it is therefore provided that in such cases it may be lawful to purchase, for ready money, in the neighbouring territories of Spain, provisions and other things necessary for the use of the garrison, the inhabitants and the ships which lie in the harbour. But if any goods be found imported by Gibraltar, either by way of barter for purchasing provisions, or under any other pretence, the same shall be confiscated, and complaint being made thereof, those persons who have acted contrary to the faith of this country, shall be severely punished. And Her Britannic Majesty at the request of the Catholic King, does consent and agree, that no leave shall be given under any pretence whatsoever, either to Jews or Moors, to reside or have their dwellings in the said town of Gibraltar; and that no refuge or shelter shall be allowed to any Moorish ships of war in the harbour of the said town, whereby the communication between Spain and Ceuta may be obstructed, or the coasts of Spain be infested by the excursions of the Moors. But whereas treaties of friendship and a liberty and intercourse of commerce are between the British and certain territories situate on the coast of Africa, it is always to be understood, that the British subjects cannot refuse the Moors and their ships entry into the port of Gibraltar purely upon the account of merchandising. Her Majesty the Queen of Great Britain does further promise, that the free exercise of their religion shall be indulged to the Roman Catholic inhabitants of the aforesaid town. And in case it shall hereafter seem meet to the Crown of Great Britain to grant, sell, or by any means to alienate therefrom the propriety of the said town of Gibraltar, it is hereby agreed, and concluded, that the preference of having the same shall always be given to the Crown of Spain before any others.

# BIBLIOGRAPHY

GENERAL WORKS

ABBOTT, W. C. *Documents Relating to the International Status of Gibraltar* (New York, 1934)

ANDREWS, ALLEN. *Proud Fortress*

AYALA, IGNACIA LOPEZ DE. *Historia de Gibraltar* (Madrid, 1782)

BAILEY, SIR EDWARD. 'Gibraltar and the Northern Rif', *Quarterly Journal of the Geological Society of London*, Vol 108 (1952), 157-75

BRADFORD, ERNIE. *Gibraltar*

BUXTON, H. J. *Mediterranean Window*

CARRINGTON, C. E. *Gibraltar – The Rock with an Emotional Problem*, Chatham House Memorandum (Oxford, 1956)

CARTER, F. *A Journey from Madrid to Malaga in 1780*

CONN, S. *Gibraltar in British Diplomacy in the Eighteenth Century*

DENNIS, P. W. C. 'Gibraltar', *Scottish Geographical Magazine*, Vol 55 (1939), 331-40

DRINKWATER, JOHN. *A History of the Late Siege of Gibraltar*

DUNCAN, FRANCIS. *History of the Royal Artillery*

ELLICOTT, DOROTHY. *Bastion Against Aggression* (Gibraltar, 1968)

——. *Gibraltar's Royal Governor* (Gibraltar, 1961)

——. 'Tarik's Hill', *Commonwealth and Empire Annual* (1953), 7-16 and 185-8

ELLICOTT, J. T. and D. M. *An Ornament to the Almeida* (Portsmouth, 1950)

FANSHAWE, ADMIRAL SIR EDWARD. *Sir Hew Dalrymple at Gibraltar*

FIELD, HENRY. *Gibraltar*

FISHER, JAMES. *Watching Birds* (Harmondsworth, 1941)

GARDINER, SIR ROBERT. *Report to Lord Palmerston*

*Gibraltar Chronicle*. Various weekly and daily editions from 1801

Gibraltar Garrison Library. *Gibraltar Directories* (Gibraltar, 1881, 1937 and 1938)

——. *Ups and Downs of the Royal Calpe Hunt* (Gibraltar, 1912)

——. *Wild Flowers of Gibraltar and the Neighbourhood* (Gibraltar, 1968)

GONZALES, A. 'History of the Gibraltar Dockyard', *Journal of the Gibraltar Society*, Vol 1 (1930), 26-52

HILLS, GEORGE. *Rock of Contention*

HORT, R. *The Rock*

HOWES, DR H. W. *The Gibraltarian*

# BIBLIOGRAPHY

HUGHES, B. P. *British Smooth Bore Artillery*
IRBY, HOWARD L. *Ornithology of the Straits of Gibraltar*
JAMES, COLONEL THOMAS. *History of the Herculean Straits*
JONES, MAURICE. *History of Coast Artillery in the British Army*
KENYON, MAJOR-GENERAL E. R. *Gibraltar under Moor, Spaniard and Briton*
LAWSON, DON. *The Lion and the Rock*
LEWINGTON, W. J. *Impeachment of Gibraltar as a Fortress*
LUDWIG, EMIL. *The Mediterranean*
McGUFFIE, T. H. *The Siege of Gibraltar*
MANN, J. H. *Gibraltar and its Sieges*
MILLER, F. F. 'Romero de Figueroa', *Journal of the Gibraltar Society*, Vol 1 (1930), 15-25
OVE ARUP and Partners. *Gibraltar Groundwater Survey 1971*
OWEN, CHARLES. *The Maltese Islands* (Newton Abbot, 1969)
PACK, S. W. C. *Sea Power in the Mediterranean*
RAMSAY, A. C. and GEIKIE, J. 'Gibraltar', *Quarterly Journal of the Geological Society of London*, Vol 34 (1878), 505-41
RODRIGUEZ, J. L. *The Story of Gibraltar and Her Stamps*
RUSSELL, JACK. *Gibraltar Besieged*
RYAN, E. F. E. *Something about Gibraltar*
SAYER, CAPTAIN. *History of Gibraltar*
Service Publications Ltd. *Gibraltar Guide*
STEWART, JOHN D. *Gibraltar the Keystone*
TAYLOR, ERNEST R. *Padre Brown of Gibraltar*
TUKE, LT-COLONEL A. J. S. *Birds of Southern Spain and Gibraltar*
WILSON, W. H. 'Tunnelling on the Rock', *Institute of Mining and Metallurgy Journal*, Vol 55 (1945-6), 193-269

### GOVERNMENT PUBLICATIONS

| | |
|---|---|
| Gibraltar Government. | *Annual Reports* (1957-72) |
| | *Census Report* (1970) |
| | *Estimates* (1974-5) |
| | *Laws of Gibraltar* (1964 Edition and Amendments) |
| | *Port Department Report* (1973) |
| Spanish Government. | *Gibraltar, Spain's Point of View* (Madrid 1974) |
| | *Negotiations on Gibraltar* (Madrid, 1968) |
| | *The Spanish Red Book* (Madrid, 1965) |
| United Kingdom Government. | *Further Documents* (HMSO, 1968) |
| | *Recent Differences with Spain* (HMSO, 1965) |
| | *Talks with Spain* (HMSO, 1966) |

# ACKNOWLEDGEMENTS

MUCH information has been obtained from the works mentioned in the bibliography. Military and political history is fully covered in these works, but it has been necessary to consult many individuals, too numerous to mention by name, about other aspects of Gibraltar. Ministers and civil servants of the Government of Gibraltar have been most helpful, especially Mr Joe Ballantine, who very kindly spent much time in making arrangements in Gibraltar on behalf of the author. The staff of the Garrison Library and many other persons in Gibraltar also gave great assistance.

In the United Kingdom help was obtained from the library of the Royal Commonwealth Society, the Public Records Office, the Royal Artillery Institute, the Gibraltar Tourist Office and the Spanish Embassy, among other organisations and persons. Mention should also be made of the kind loan of many books and papers by Mr Michael Brufal.

Lastly, the publishers and author are most grateful to the Gibraltar Tourist Office for the photographs marked *GTO*, to the *Gibraltar Chronicle* for those marked *GC*, to *The Times* for the photograph of the harbour, and to Mr Charles Perez for his photographs of birds.

# INDEX